WHAT THEY'RE SAYING ...

"**N**othing compares to riding your bike down a country road. Suddenly you're free of all cares and concerns and totally absorbed in the moment. Your senses come alive. Sights, sounds, and smells heighten your appreciation of the nature surrounding you. *Bicycling Southern New Hampshire* is a perfect guide to your escape from the humdrum and to reawaken what really is important—your mental and physical well-being. Ride along with Linda Chestney—you'll be glad you did!"

—**Barbara Siegert, author of *Bicycle Across America***

"**O**nce again Linda Chestney has authored an excellent book for the touring cyclist, and families as well. The personal touch included with the ride descriptions helps the reader know what to expect around the next turn.

Southern New Hampshire has many delightful areas in which to cycle. Linda's new book will help you experience them to the fullest."

—**Dave Topham, League of American Bicyclist NH rep., charter member Granite State Wheelman**

"**B**icyclists visiting New Hampshire often pay hundreds, if not thousands of dollars for a guided cycling tour. With Linda Chestney's book, cyclists now have the best rides in New Hampshire—and probably New England—at their fingertips for just a few bucks!

The rides in this book offer something for bicycle riders of all levels—from relaxed jaunts of a few miles to day-long banquets through New Hampshire's amazing countryside. Each ride has its own unique characteristics and offerings. Ride them all. Cycling just doesn't get any better than this!"

—**Roger Turner, NH Cycling Club, all-year-long crazy cyclist, 1999 First Place Winner Concord (NH) Criterium (Age 45+ category)**

"**A**n excellent source for all cyclists. The rides provide terrific scenery and a mixed-bag terrain, suitable for all abilities. Some of the best cycling you'll find, and it's right in our back yard. Whether you're an athlete-in-training or the weekend enthusiast, this book is for you!"
—**Michael Cropper, endurance athlete, 1999 Ironman USA finisher**

"**E**ven though New Hampshire has more rail-trails per capita than any other state in the nation, when you come off that extensive network, you need a credible and well laid-out book that focuses on the local opportunities for on-road riding, and information on where to go, where to eat, etc.

Linda Chestney's newest work, *Bicycling Southern New Hampshire*, fills that need admirably. Not only does this beautifully written book give you some needed and pertinent clues into New Hampshire's extensive backroads, but it also gives you a sense of the grandeur and timelessness of this Currier & Ives area of New England."
—**Craig P. Della Penna, New England rep for Rails-to-Trails Conservancy, and author of *Great Rail-Trails of Southern New England***

"**A**s a New Hampshire resident and cycling enthusiast, I have enjoyed many miles, and many years on the open road. Yet, you rarely know what is in your own back yard. When we want to get away for a while, we select a bike tour new to us, load up our bikes, and soon find ourselves zipping down backroads that are far closer than we realize—many in our own back yard.

Linda Chestney brings the adventure of New Hampshire's back roads to us. Breathtaking vistas, tranquil country roads, and unique discoveries lie just around every bend in the road. Many jewels are to be found on your New Hampshire outdoor riding ventures. Whether you are visitor to New Hampshire, or a resident, *Bicycling Southern New Hampshire* will take you get there. See you on the road!"
—**Krystina Deren Arrain, East Coast Greenway Alliance/NH**

BICYCLING

Southern
New Hampshire

BICYCLING

Southern
New Hampshire

Second Editon
Completely Revised and Expanded

Linda Chestney

NICOLIN FIELDS
PUBLISHING
INCORPORATED

North Hampton, New Hampshire

First Printing, March 1994
Second Printing, June 1994
Third Printing, August 1996
Fourth Printing, completely revised, March 2000

Cover design © by Kim Robert Nilsen
Maps © by R.P. Hale
Photos © by Linda Chestney, unless noted otherwise
Printed in the United States of America

Library of Congress Cataloging-in-Publication Data

Chestney, Linda, 1952–
    Bicycling southern New Hampshire / Linda Chestney. -- 2nd ed., completely rev. and expanded.
    p. cm.
    Rev. ed. of: Cycling the backroads of southern New Hampshire. 1st ed. c1994.
    ISBN 0-9637077-5-2 (pbk.)
    1. Bicycle touring--New Hampshire--Guidebooks. 2. New Hampshire--Guidebooks. 3. Rural roads--New Hampshire--Guidebooks. I. Chestney, Linda, 1952- Cycling the backroads of southern New Hampshire. II. Title.
    GV1045.5.N4 C47 2000
    917.42--dc21

                                    99-086479

For my fellow pedaler,
my "bestest" buddy,
my pearl among the pebbles,
my husband,
Al Blake
~Truly, the best wine was saved for last.

Acknowledgments

My thanks to the many, many people who helped make this book a reality. A very special thanks to "Baby Doc" Cindy Hoover, who lit the initial fire many years ago, and kept it burning with her gentle prodding of "andalé, andalé" on those oh, so many bike rides. I'm grateful for her long-term friendship over many years and many miles!

Thank you to the people who offered new rides to include in this revised, expanded edition. Thanks to Mike Cropper for the Hampton Beach-Exeter ride, Barbara Siegert and Joan Drapeau for the Newmarket rides, Jim Venne for the Stratham-Rye tour and his valuable work with MS bike rides, Krystina Arrain for the Rochester-Lebanon, ME ride, Cameron Wake for his work on the new bike-ped SABR-bridge included in his Portsmouth-Newington ride, Dennis Meadows for his excellent changes on the Exeter-Durham ride, Ken Richardson for the fabulous Gilmanton-Loudon ride, Roger Turner for the terrific New Boston-Greenfield ride. And also a big thank you to Dave Topham for suggesting the Salem-Hampstead ride, as well as offering some excellent safety and cycling tips. A big thank you, too, to Roger C. Parker for his superb advice.

The exceptional natural talent of Kim Robert Nilsen, the cover artist, I also gratefully acknowledge. Kim, thanks for filling in the gap.

And Now Your Input...

If there's one constant in life, it's change. This book is no exception. Perhaps when you ride one of these tours, changes will have occurred in road signs, business establishments, landmarks, etc. Let us know of these changes.

Also, if you have an idea for improving a ride, or if you have a favorite ride you'd like to see included in a future edition, please drop us a note. We'd love to consider it. Send your note to: Publisher, Nicolin Fields Publishing, Inc., 3 Red Fox Road, North Hampton, NH, 03862. Phone 603 964-1727, or email at nfp@nh.ultranet.com. Web site at www.NicolinFields.com.

C3C3C3

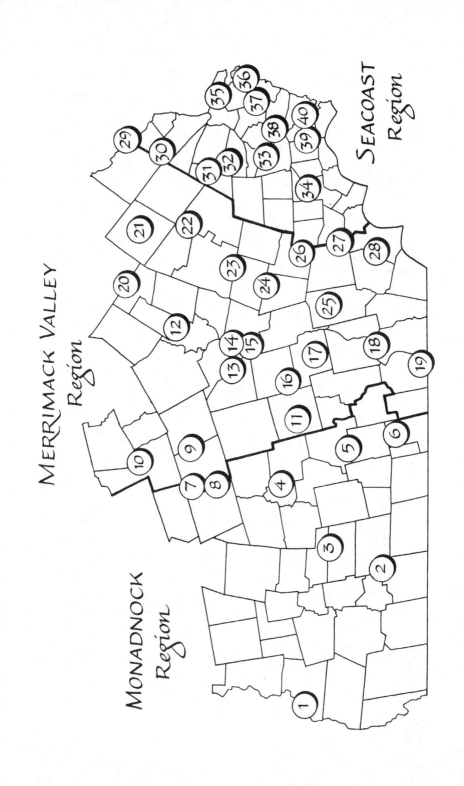

Contents

Bicycling Southern New Hampshire

*Just specimens is all New
Hampshire has,
One each of everything
as in a showcase,
which naturally she
doesn't care to sell.*

— Robert Frost, *"New Hampshire"* 1923

As Robert Frost notes, New Hampshire has "one of everything, which she doesn't care to sell." But she doesn't mind sharing. New Hampshire, as Robert Frost alludes to, is its own found paradise. There's a little bit of everything here. Rich history. Classic architecture. Spectacular scenery. Warm people. And lots of backroads that meander through countryside—perfect for cycling.

If you're looking for a family activity—a chance for everyone to do something together—to have some fun, stop for a picnic or jump in the old swimming hole, New Hampshire cycling can't be beat. No matter what your age or skill level, male or female, you can find pleasure in cycling. Whether you're a racer or a "let's take 'er easy" rider, you'll find New Hampshire has something to meet your cycling needs. Come on, get out your bike, dust it off and join in the fun of cycling the classic scenery of southern New Hampshire!

Uniquely Southern New Hampshire

Bicycling Southern New Hampshire is the first guide specifically written for cycling in southern New Hampshire. This is the completely revised, expanded edition. We've added over a dozen more rides to the many favorites which were recorded in the first edition. Although other books offer great rides in the White Mountains and Lakes region, many people object to traveling two hours or more by car for a bike ride. Enter *Bicycling Southern New Hampshire*. For those who live in southern New Hampshire, those visiting from out-of-state, those who don't have the time, or those who are simply unwilling to travel a couple of hours or so for a ride, this book provides ready-made, easy-to-get-to tours.

The rides are designed to keep you off the busy roads and introduce you to the serenity of New Hampshire backroads. Occasionally however, a busier road is used because it's unavoidable or designed to take you past a point of interest. All the tours begin at point A, loop around, and bring you back to point A.

A Mole Hill or Mount Everest?

The rides in this book range from 9.5 to 103.8 miles. Most are 20+ miles. They span the gamut from beginner level, intermediate to more experienced cycling—with the majority of rides in the intermediate range. Some rides are ideal for family riding—choose one with fewer miles.

And of course, there's the expert level—more challenging rides with steeper hills and longer distances—like the Tri-State Century West. It's a 103.8-mile ride that can be done in a day, but two days may better suit your style.

Bear in mind, this *is* New Hampshire, and there *are* hills here. They're unavoidable. If you find a hill too difficult to ride, walk it. Like any other sport, you get better—the hills get easier—the more you do it.

These rides are for fun! So take a bag lunch or stop at an eatery along the way. Drink in the scenery. Cruise through fragrant apple orchards. Watch the grazing Holstein cattle or the great blue herons fishing. Climb to the top of Mount Kearsarge. Snap some photos of pristine New England churches. Browse through the antique shops or sit on a park bench and watch the sailboats. Enjoy!

Touring Tips

An exhilarating sport, bicycling can be enjoyed even more when some simple guidelines are observed. With a little common sense, proper equipment, and education, you'll be better prepared to enjoy a safe, fun ride.

Equipment Makes All the Difference

• **Bicycle helmets** save lives. Statistics about head injuries are staggering. A five-year study conducted by the Center for Disease Control in Atlanta indicates that nearly three million people suffer bike injuries—and almost 5,000 died—more than half from head injuries. Two of every five head injuries occurred in children under 15. Set a good example—wear a helmet.

Make sure the helmet you purchase bears the American National Standard Institute (ANSI) seal or is approved by the Snell Memorial Foundation.

• A **handlebar bag** is a good investment. It holds a lot. Some have a clear plastic map holder to place your ride map and directions in. You can carry tissues, food, wallet, etc. inside your bag. Pannier bags (saddle bags) are useful for overnight tours or if you make numerous purchases. These two bags mount on a rack over the back or front wheel. If you want to travel very light, snap a fanny pack around your waist. A wedge bag mounted underneath your seat or top tube can hold tools, wallet, spare tube, or a bike lock.

• A **computer odometer** is a necessity. It provides instant feedback on how far you've gone so you can match your odometer mileage to what's noted in the book. Then you'll know when it's time to turn. Your computer may not measure mileage exactly as this book does. Many variables affect its read-out—the amount of pressure in your tires, the size of your tires, how accurately you've calibrated your computer. In any event, the numbers will probably be close enough, along with the landmarks mentioned in the book, so you'll be able to know you're where you should be.

• A **rearview mirror** attached to your bike helmet, sunglasses, or the left side of your handlebars is a smart move. You can then watch traffic approaching from behind.

• Bring a **water bottle or** two with you. Sip water often—even before you're thirsty. Adequate hydration is important for optimal cycling efficiency.

• **Padded gloves** can absorb road shock and protect your hands from potential "road rash" should you take a tumble.

• Many people feel a **gel seat** increases cycling pleasure tenfold. It cushions your rump—undoubtedly a good investment for the "tenderfoot."

More Ideas for a Comfortable Ride

• Remember to carry items such as **tissues, sunscreen, sunglasses** with UV protection, grease clean-up packets (should your chain derail), a spare tube or tube kit, a pump, a basic repair kit, and a first-aid kit.

• To reposition a chain, remove a rear wheel, or do other "dirty work," using inexpensive throw-away (but after you get home!) **latex exam gloves** saves a lot of clean-up time. A pair of gloves will often fit easily in a 35mm film canister, and often only one glove is needed for a job.

• **Bring some cash.** You may want to stop along the way for a bite to eat, ice cream, or a shopping excursion at a craft or gift shop.

• **Food,** such as fresh fruit (cherries, bananas, oranges) or a sandwich, crackers, or energy bars are good for refueling.

Snack on something every couple of hours.

• **Dress comfortably.** Lycra clothing is very popular for cycling because it's nice and cool when riding. Its wicking effect absorbs sweat and keeps you cooler than conventional clothing. Lycra shorts are available with padding where it counts—which makes for a more comfortable ride.

But if Lycra isn't your thing—no worry—wear whatever is comfortable. But avoid pants with bulky inner seams, like blue jeans or any long-legged slacks which could catch in the chain. Use pant clips (straps) if you *do* wear slacks, or better yet, wear tights.

• A **brightly colored wind breaker** is an excellent way to enhance your visibility. Studies show that neon pink is the most effective because it is not the color of road signs or emergency vehicles and it's the most unexpected color for a motorist to encounter.

• Pick up an inexpensive plastic **rain poncho** that tucks into a packet about four inches square and throw it in your bike bag. New England weather is unpredictable.

Travel Smart Safety Tips

• **It's the law.** Cyclists are governed by the same rules of the road as motorists. And yes, in this state you *can* get a ticket if you disobey the law while on your bike. Follow the same rules as for driving. Ride *with* the traffic. Signal your intentions. Stop at stop signs. Don't ride on the sidewalk.

• Ride **single file.** Ride confidently to communicate to motorists you are a competent cyclist. We need to earn their respect. Too many uneducated cyclists continue to tarnish cyclists' image with annoying and unsafe behavior such as riding two abreast or on the wrong side of the road.

• Always carry **identification**—a business card or index card with your name, address, phone number, and information about who to call should you have an accident. Let someone know where you're going.

• The water bottle is also a handy deterrent for nasty **dogs**. Squirting a dog with water will startle it, and often cause it to stop its aggressive behavior.

Other suggestions for avoiding **territorial dogs**, try the "holler and point" trick. Shout "Get back there!" or "Go lie down!" They'll often leave you alone. Most bike-dog injuries to cyclists occur because the dog is hit by the bike, or by cyclists losing control swinging a bike pump, (or whatever) trying to defend themselves. If the "point and holler" approach doesn't work, get off your bike and position the bike between you and the dog as you walk briskly out of their territory. When there is no challenge of a chase, almost all dogs will become disinterested and go home.

• **Avoid riding in sand**—it can cause a nasty tumble. Be very careful when crossing railroad tracks. Cross them on a perpendicular. Be on the lookout for storm grates. They can cause serious falls. Also use extreme caution on steel-decked bridges and painted surfaces, especially when they are wet.

• **Pace your ride.** Don't take on rides beyond your ability. On long rides, begin slowly. Stop frequently to stretch and walk about. These breaks will prolong your stamina and allow longer, more comfortable rides.

• **Don't use headphones** while you're riding. You'll need total concentration to be aware of traffic hazards.

Join a Club

Cycling is often more enjoyable when it's shared. If you live in New Hampshire, join a touring club. The largest in the state, Granite State Wheelmen, is open to anyone interested in bicycling. Organized rides are scheduled nearly every evening in the summer, spring and fall. And for the hardier, winter rides are available.

The club also hosts a yearly Tri-State Seacoast Century in September. Yes, that's 100 miles in one day! But you can choose to do 25, 50, or 75 miles instead. It's great fun and you can get a patch that says you really did ride 100 miles!

Different levels of cycling skills are also considered, so you can choose one that's appropriate to your abilities. The club recently added "turtle rides" for the slower-paced, leisure rider. It's fun, and a great way to meet others who love the sport. For membership information, pick up one of their brochures at any bicycle shop, call 603 898-5479, or write GSW, PMB 216, 215 So. Broadway, Salem, NH 03079.

The League of American Bicyclist is a national organization for bicyclists, formed in 1880. It promotes bicycling for recreation, transportation and fitness, and educates the public on issues concerning safe and effective bicycling. It conducts advocacy work for the full rights of bicyclists. For more information, write to them at 1612 K Street NW, Suite 401, Washington, DC 20006, or call 202 822-1333.

How to Use This Book

Bicycling Southern New Hampshire indicates the number of miles and a description of the ride at the beginning of each chapter. The number of miles will increase the difficulty just because the more miles you do, the more potential for fatigue to set in.

Evaluate that along with the ride's description (hilly, flat, rolling) and make your decision. Don't forego a ride however, just because it has some hills. Walking is ok. You're still out there getting exercise and enjoying the scenery. And what better way to impress your friends than to say, "Yeah, I knocked off 27 miles on my bike today."

So get on your bike, shove off, and be prepared to experience the backroads of southern New Hampshire at their best.

C8C8C8

MONADNOCK REGION

1 TRI–STATE CENTURY WEST

103.8 miles
Challenging—because it's a long ride,
rolling, with three, long, difficult climbs.

More rolling countryside, white-steepled churches, and town meeting houses on village greens? More crystalline lakes, winding roads, and breath-taking views? More... well, I'm afraid it can't be avoided. This is classic New England, folks, complete with all the visual clichés.

The area this tour covers—a small section of Massachusetts, the Monadnock region of New Hampshire and adjacent southern Vermont—is known as the Currier and Ives corner of New England. It's no wonder. It's truly picture perfect. Miles and miles of road snake along the scenic Connecticut River Valley. As early morning fog lifts, cattle low in dairy barns. The sun penetrates trees overhead, creating lacy patterns on road surfaces. Less-traveled backroads meander through colonial villages that ignore time's passage. A pumpkin patch the Great Pumpkin undoubtedly smiles upon spills orange across an otherwise green palette. New England. There's no better way to appreciate the gift of beauty New England offers than from the saddle of a bicycle—here in this Currier and Ives setting.

The tour begins in Westmoreland, New Hampshire—a quiet, peaceful village with a town green, a historic meeting house and the unpretentious charm of a small colonial village. It's like taking a step back in time. Westmoreland is the home of Park Hill Meeting House, a magnificent structure built in 1762. Considered one of the most beautiful churches in New England, it was added to the National Register in 1980. Situated on a sloping green on Park Hill Common, where its gilded weather vane sweeps the sky, the building boasts a steeple with a Palladian window and a bell cast by the Paul Revere Foundry.

Newfane, one of the most-photographed towns in Vermont, is the half-way point in the ride. This pretty village in the Green Mountains has grown little since the 18th century. Teddy Roosevelt was once a visitor; now the economist John Kenneth Galbraith is its most prominent summer resident. During the fall Newfane's shaded green with its white Congregational Church, Greek Revival courthouse and old inns, is ablaze of color as the leaves change from green to varying shades of red, gold, orange, and russet.

Although this is a century ride (100 miles) it can be split into two days. Hardy souls can do it in a day (the author did and lived to tell about it!). But most prefer to make a weekend of it. There are overnight accommodations near the start of the trip as well as at the half-way point (see Ride Information).

An excellent place for breakfast before you begin your ride, Stuart and John's Sugar House and Pancake Restaurant is immediately on the left as you turn on Route 63S. They promise genuine made-in-New-Hampshire maple syrup and a hardy send-off. (See additional information under 99.9 miles.)

RIDE INFORMATION

Highlights: Numerous historic markers, Park Hill Meeting House, scenic views along the Connecticut River, herds of Holsteins grazing on verdant hillsides, sheep and llama farms, serene mountain views, lots of antique shops, a swimming hole, and even a covered bridge.

Start: Westmoreland town green. To get there take Route 101 to Route 12N in Keene. Follow Route 12N to Route 63S. Left on 63S for four miles to Westmoreland center. Park on the left end of the United Church's Fellowship Hall parking lot.

Lodging: You can stay at the Chesterfield House Inn (603 256-3211) in West Chesterfield the night before the ride. Or check with Keene Chamber of Commerce (352-1303) for other suggestions. Halfway, consider staying at River Bend Lodge (802 365-7952). It's just beyond Newfane (VT). Inns in Newfane tend to be pricey or unwilling to accommodate guests for one night only, but pick up a book on Vermont inns or call information.

RIDE DIRECTIONS

0.0 **Left on Route 63S.**

At 3.6 miles, Spofford Lake is on the left.

4.4 **At stop sign, go straight—still on Route 63S.**

At 5.6 miles in Chesterfield a historic marker notes Chief Justice Harlan Fiske Stone's accomplishments. Born in Chesterfield, he later served as Attorney General of the United States in Coolidge's cabinet and was appointed Chief Justice in 1941.

Many of Chesterfield's colonial buildings, churches, and homes were built in the late 1700s and mid-1800s. Their classic, fluted columns, Palladian windows, and of course, shutters, stand proudly in this quiet corner of the state.

At about 7.5 miles you begin a tough 1.5-mile climb. Hang in—the other side is a gift. You glide and glide and glide!

12.8 At stop sign, turn right on Route 63S in Hinsdale.

13.1 Left on Route 63S.

At 15.1 miles on the right, don't miss the garage that sports the latest trend in siding—license plates.

18.5 At the stop sign, turn right on Route 63S/10S to Northfield, Massachusetts.

There are several places to eat along Route 63 in Northfield.

As you cycle past, you'll notice the stately brick buildings of Northfield-Mount Herman, a private co-educational preparatory school, which borders Route 63.

21.0 Right on Route 10S. Cross the Connecticut River.

23.0 Right on Route 142N. Caution: You'll encounter three sets of railroad tracks before you reach Brattleboro. Walk your bike.

At 29.9 miles is Schoolhouse Grocery and Deli. They have great sandwiches—ham and Swiss, tuna, seafood salad, and more.

38.0 At stop sign, turn left, then an immediate right through busy downtown Brattleboro following signs for Route 30N.

At this corner is the Brattleboro Museum and Art Center. A converted railroad station, it hosts art and historical exhibits as well as an Estey organ from the days when the city was home to one of the world's largest organ companies.

Brattleboro offers many eating choices.

While in town, you may want to make a stop at Brattleboro Bicycle Shop at 165 Main Street. Priority is given to touring cyclists like you who are on extended trips. So if you need a spare tire, a replacement for a broken mirror, or the latest in Lycra, stop in.

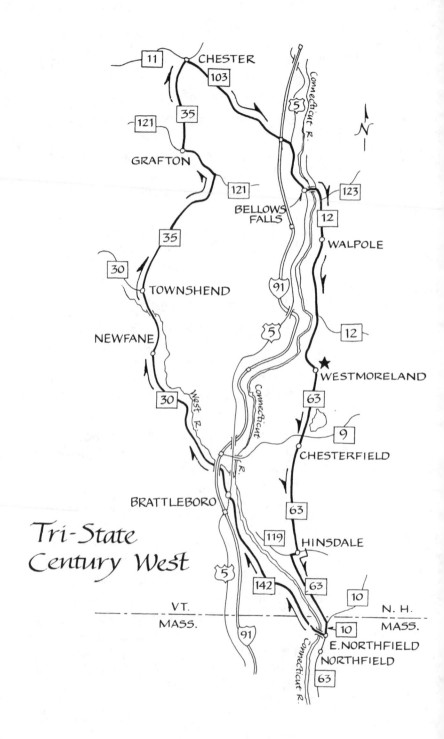

Tri-State
Century West

38.4   Left onto Route 30.

Route 30 has a wide shoulder. It follows West River. At 42.6 miles don't miss the swimming hole. The river is clean and extremely refreshing—especially if you catch it on a 90 degree day like we did!

A prime photo opportunity—a covered bridge—presents itself at 45.3 miles. Pose for the family album. It'll also help you convince your brother-in-law you really did pedal 104 miles in two days!

At the 50-mile point, you enter Newfane, Vermont. Despite its small size, it has super shops where you can find fudge, quilts, antiques, genuine Vermont maple syrup, and cheddar cheese. This is also the home of Vermont's largest flea market on Sundays in the summer.

At the 52.9-mile mark is the River Bend Lodge. It's the perfect half-way point to stay overnight—clean accommodations, reasonable rates, and a lovely country setting. There's also a restaurant next door—Coach House Ristorante—let's carbo-load!

55.2   Bear right on Route 35N in Townshend.

Enjoy this pristine town green with a gazebo, because right after it you begin a long, arduous uphill. Hang on—there's a downhill to match! And don't forget—this is fun!

Route 35 is a fabulous road with breathtaking mountain views. At about 57.4 miles on the right is a llama farm.

65.6   Bear left on Route 35N.

69.5   Right—still on Route 35N in Grafton.

Begin a long, difficult uphill.

Grafton is one of Vermont's prettiest villages. It has undergone much restoration in recent years.

One of its finest buildings is the Old Tavern, an inn visited by figures as diverse as Henry David Thoreau, Daniel Webster, and more recently, Paul Newman and Joanne Woodward.

76.8 **At stop sign, go right on 103S in Chester, Vermont.**
The famous Vermont Country Store is at 83.9 miles. It's worth a stop just to check out their quirky inventory!

86.2 **Straight on Route 5S toward Bellows Falls.**

89.5 **At Y, turn left. Stay on Route 5 through downtown Bellows Falls.**

90.0 **At intersection with brick building straight ahead, go left. Cross two bridges.**
At this location the first canal in the U.S. was built in 1802.

90.3 **At stop light, turn right on Route 12S.**
You're back in New Hampshire. A couple of miles down the road on the right is Diamond Pizza. People travel miles for their pizzas!

99.9 **Right on Route 63S.**
At the 100.1-mile point is Stuart and John's Sugar House and Pancake Restaurant, where plain, blueberry, or chocolate chip pancakes slathered with pure maple sugar satiate your desire for down-home cookin'! Open weekends 7 a.m.–3 p.m.

Historic Park Hill Meeting House is located at the 102.5-mile point.

103.8 **Back at Westmoreland where you began.**

2 TROY–RINDGE

27.3 miles
Hilly, some steep hills, one long,
hill, for the seasoned cyclist—because
of busy roads or no shoulders

Irresistibly New England, unquestionably New Hampshire—this is the Monadnock region—the Currier and Ives corner of New England. Replete with white church steeples climbing high above the trees, and winding roads that command a more leisurely pace with hundreds of miles of less-traveled backroads, this region is pure delight for cyclists.

Here rolling countryside is dominated by the 3,165- foot mountain for which the region is named. You'll periodically see majestic Mount Monadnock looming in the distance as you travel.

This tour takes you past Cathedral of the Pines, an outdoor shrine where all may worship. The cathedral was established as a lasting memorial to martyrs of American wars. Visited by millions of people, groups as different as the Kiwanis, motorcycle clubs, and Hindus come to conduct services throughout the summer.

Along Route 124, you pedal past farms with grazing Holstein cattle, stone walls, and the sweet smell of silage. You pass several magnificent colonial homes with white picket fences and attached barns. Don't miss the unique weather vanes atop barns and churches along the way.

RIDE INFORMATION

Highlights: Cathedral of the Pines, Annett State Park, Monadnock State Park, examples of classic colonial architecture, hiking trails, and shopping—baskets, wooden products, antiques.

Start: Strip mall on Route 12 in Troy that has a Minute Mart Convenience Store, a post office and restaurant. To get there, take Route 101 to Route 12S to Troy center.

RIDE DIRECTIONS

0.0   **Left out of the parking lot to stop sign. At stop sign, go left on Route 12S, keep the common on the left.** The small, white Gothic gazebo near the war monuments on the common is a super place to have a picnic lunch after your ride.

0.4   **At end of common, go left—still on Route 12S. (A bakery is in front of you just before the turn.)** Route 12S has fast, busy traffic with a wide breakdown area. It's mostly flat with one long, moderate climb.

As you leave Troy there are a number of early and mid-1800s Federal-style homes with pillars, black shutters, wood-carved door lintels, or granite window and door lintels. The elliptical fanlights over paneled doors and the brick or clapboard facades exhibit the detailed elegance of days past.

4.4   **At the yellow blinker, turn left on Route 119E.** This road has fast traffic, no breakdown.

A right at this Route 119 intersection takes you to Rhododendron State Park. It's worth a side trip in mid-July when the 16 acres of wild rhododendrons are at their finest.

At 7.5 miles there's a marsh on your right. Keep an eye out for occasional great blue herons and Canada geese.

9.9 **At stop light, go straight on Route 119E.**
To enjoy a lovely restaurant and inn that people travel from all over to visit, go left at this light to Woodbound Inn.

If historic small towns enthrall you, take a right at 11.0 miles by the yellow blinker to Rindge Center where you'll find the Meeting House built in 1796, several 1700s and 1800s sawmills, gristmills, and tanneries on streams, and Rindge Historical Society Museum at the town library where a fascinating array of samplers, muskets, stuffed birds, a soldier's discharge letter signed by General George Washington, and other historical artifacts are on display.

11.5 **At yellow blinker, turn left on Cathedral Road, which has no shoulder, and light, fast traffic. There's an "Annett State Park" sign at this corner.**
The entrance to Cathedral of the Pines is on your left at about 13.1 miles. Shortly after that—at 14.1 miles—is the entrance to Annett State Park—a perfect place for a picnic lunch.

14.6 **At Y, turn right on Prescott Road.**
Just after the Y on the right is a stately double-chimneyed, Federal-style home with black shutters, a white-columned portico, and a fanlight over the front door flanked by detailed rosette carvings. This house, built circa 1825, is framed by large, dignified maple trees.

15.2 **At the stop sign, turn left on Turnpike Road (Route 124W).** This is a busy road that's rolling with a couple steep, uphill climbs. The shoulder appears and disappears.

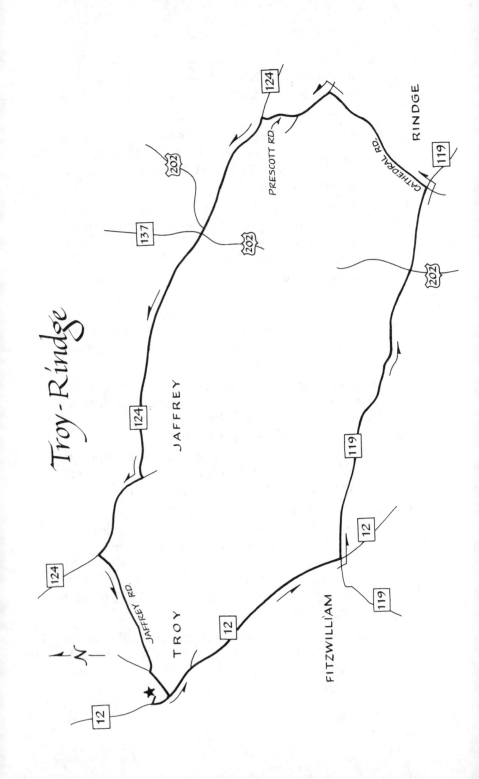

Troy-Rindge

For ice cream, stop at Kimball Farm Restaurant at about 16.6 miles.

Mt. Monadnock looms in the distance here, as you glance west.

17.4   At stop light in Jaffrey—go straight on Rte. 124W.
In Jaffrey village, there are numerous places for lunch. If you'd like to stop for a rest, consider the common, where a delightful gazebo and numerous park benches adorn the lawn. Take in the Jaffrey Historical Society if you're a history buff. Don't miss the classic colonial architecture of St. Patrick's church with its fieldstone construction and multi-arched windows, or shortly after it— the classic colonial United Church of Jaffrey. Also of interest is the Cutler Memorial Building with its splendid clock tower. If your timing is right, you'll hear it gong the hour. ·

If you have chosen to make this a two-day tour, you may want to end today's ride at 19.2 miles and stay overnight at the Inn at Jaffrey Center, or at the very least, indulge in an elegant lunch.

Another wonderful colonial church, the First Church of Jaffrey, looms on the hill in Jaffrey Center on your right at about 19.4 miles. The charm of old New England is captured timeless in its white clock tower, four-tiered steeple, 12-over-12 windows, and charming weather vane. Two other historical sites are in this area—the Old Meeting House and the Little Red Schoolhouse.

If you brought your lunch, plan to picnic at Monadnock State Park. The turn-off is on your right at about 19.7 miles. Camp, bird watch, or hike to your heart's delight.

At 21.8 miles a glance to the right presents a great view of Mount Monadnock. If you're ambitious, hike the trail at the 22.7 mile point.

24.0   Left by sign that says, "The Inn at East Hill Farm."
There's one short, steep hill after the turn. This rolling, tree-lined road boasts stone walls and stately colonial homes with double chimneys.

26.8   At stop sign, turn right on Route 12.
From this stop sign you have a great view of the handsome Troy Baptist Church. Built in 1789, it's an architectural jewel made of brick with classic white pillars, Gothic-arched windows, and a layered steeple.

27.0   At Y, bear right on Route 12 for 0.2 mile and then at 27.2 bear right by strip mall.

27.3   Right into parking lot where you began your tour.

3 DUBLIN–HARRISVILLE

14.5 miles
Rolling, gradual inclines, one short,
steep hill, two miles of well-packed
gravel, and lots of downhills

To appreciate the special nature of the Mount Monadnock region, you have to experience its geography and picturesque landscape. Despite its modest size, the Monadnock region is especially rich in cultural and intellectual events—concerts, plays, films, and workshops. Country stores and antique shops add a special flavor to the region, as do the huge network of secondary roads for cycling. The area straddles history by containing everything from old saltbox homes to the high-tech electronics publishing industry.

A nice family tour, this ride begins in Dublin, a charming rural town settled in the mid-1700s by Scotch colonists. One of the earliest New England resorts, it attracted such writers as Emerson, Longfellow, Thoreau, and Twain. The town has resplendent Federal houses, a handsome Community Church with Ionic columns, and a stately town hall with a Palladian window. At Yankee Books on Main Street, browse through a vast inventory of books for sale. Also downtown Dublin is a historic marker on the site of Joseph Appleton's store where in 1825 you could buy Medford Rum for three cents a glass with sugar, two cents without.

You travel on to Harrisville, one of the most perfectly preserved 19th-century New England mill towns, and also one of the prettiest—with its brick mill buildings gathered

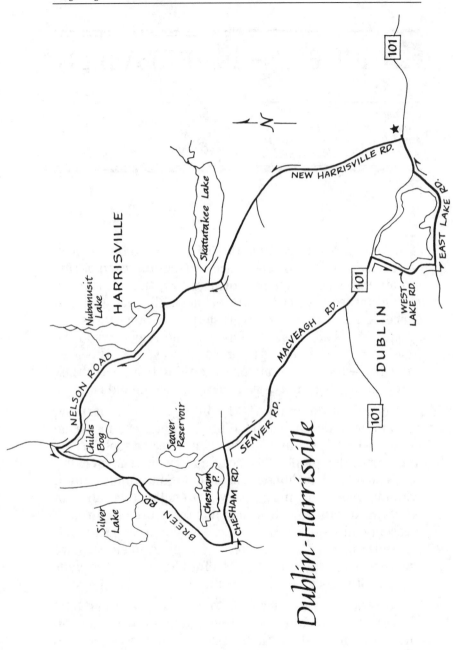

along Harrisville Pond. A National Historic Landmark, the quiet mill village is a classic jewel with its timeless architecture and seven lakes and ponds. The slower pace of life draws visitors who triple the population during the summer.

RIDE INFORMATION

Highlights: A super family tour (a short ride with little traffic and lots of attractions), The Friendly Farm, Monadnock State Park, Harrisville (the historic mill town), and historic markers.

Start: Yankee Books parking lot on Main Street/ Route 101 by the Dublin Fire Station in Dublin.

RIDE DIRECTIONS

0.0 **Right out of the parking lot a short way and then turn right on New Harrisville Road.**

A short walk down by the mill area in Harrisville village reveals a great view of the town and its one granite factory. Yes, the cupola on the factory tower is actually crooked.

"A Walking Tour of Harrisville," brochure is available at Harrisville Designs Weaving Center, where they manufacture looms and yarns and serve as an education center for workshops taught by instructors from around the world.

3.8 **At Y, go right on Nelson Road.**

This tree-lined country road, where the sun shines through the leaves and creates lacy patterns on the pavement, skirts Nubanusit Lake. Soon you'll see Child's Bog through thick woods on the left.

5.8 **Left on Breen Road.**

This tree-lined road with virtually no traffic offers nice mountain views. Silver Lake Beach is great for a picnic.

8.2 **At stop sign, turn left on Chesham Road.**
Chesham Pond appears on the left. At 8.5 miles
a small dam offers another lunch spot.

9.3 **Right on Seaver Road where there's an immediate steep uphill. You'll travel on hard-packed gravel for a couple of miles.**

9.7 **Stop sign. Stay straight, now on MacVeagh Road.**
You'll catch glimpses of Mount Monadnock on
this road.

11.5 **Left on Route 101E (unmarked).**
This road has fast traffic, but a generous shoulder, too. After this turn, the Friendly Farm is on
the right. Children love to pat and feed the lambs,
kids, fawns, chicks, and rabbits. Open daily 10–5
(weather permitting) from May to Labor Day,
weekends through mid-October. Admission fee.

12.1 **Right on West Lake Road around Dublin Pond.**
The real estate around this pond is magnificent—
mansions with ivy-covered stone walls, brick
structures, and cedar-shingled boat houses nicer
than some homes.

12.9 **At stop sign, left on East Lake Road.**

14.1 **Right on Route 101E.**
At 14.1 miles there's a right turn for Monadnock
State Park. Mount Monadnock, a mecca for hikers and one of the single most-climbed mountains in North America, offers 40 miles of trails
leading to its 3,165 foot summit, where on a clear
day you can see the Atlantic Ocean and Boston.

Don't miss the interesting buildings in Dublin
center—the Dublin Town Hall (1882) with its
classic columns and Palladian window and the
town library built of fieldstone.

14.5 **Dublin Fire Station parking lot is on the left.**

4 FRANCESTOWN– BENNINGTON

22.5 miles
Rolling, with a few long hills

They don't get any better than this, folks. This is the ultimate in classic New England. All the clichés are here—fabulous mountain views, covered bridges, historic New England structures, picturesque birch stands, and of course, the perfect backdrop for autumn colors, stone walls.

One of the eastern most towns in the Monadnock region, Francestown (incorporated 1772), is a small New England village that exudes a rustic beauty. Surrounded by hilly, wooded land, it was a mercantile town in colonial days. A historic marker notes the discovery of soapstone by Daniel Fuller, who quarried it for use in sinks, water pipes, stoves, warming stones, and mantels. Other commerce included grist, bobbins, oil, saw, and cider mills. Tanners, tailors, hatters, wheelwrights, smiths, and cabinetmakers were also found here in days gone by.

But this quiet town with its grandiose Federal-style homes is best known for its cultivation of academic excellence in the form of Francestown Academy. Both fourteenth President Franklin Pierce, and Levi Woodbury, Supreme Court justice, Navy and Treasury Secretary, graduated from the academy. This academy at the southern end of town closed in 1921. It now serves as the town hall. It's the well-kept structure with the cupola atop.

The tour begins by Francestown Village Store—an institution in the village since 1814. Across the street from it is a historic home—the Uriah Smith House, built in 1819. Also noteworthy is the Community Church with its red doors and unique weather vane.

The ride continues through the small villages of Greenfield, Hancock, and Bennington, skirts Crotched Mountain, and returns to Francestown. In Greenfield you'll pass the oldest original meeting house in New Hampshire serving both church and state. The simple clapboard structure, built in 1795, still serves the Greenfield community. The Greenfield Meeting House was listed on the National Register in 1983.

RIDE INFORMATION

Highlights: Historic markers, historic meeting house, covered bridge, and Greenfield State Park for picnicking, hiking, or swimming. A super family ride—just walk your bikes up the hills.

Start: Francestown center. Take scenic Route 136 to Francestown and park on Route 47 near Francestown Village Store.

RIDE DIRECTIONS

0.0 Take Route 47S.
(If you're facing the Francestown Village Store, you'll want to go right—toward the white spire above the trees.) Sparse traffic.

0.1 Bear right at fork on Route 136W toward Greenfield.
At this corner is the former Francestown Academy and a war monument.

4.6 In Greenfield, turn right on Route 136W intersection by a country store. Caution: Railroad tracks at 5.1 miles.

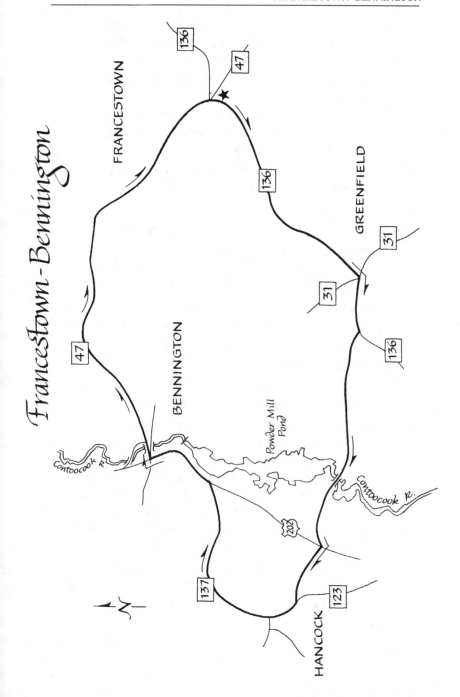

Francestown - Bennington

FRANCESTOWN

GREENFIELD

BENNINGTON

HANCOCK

Powder Mill Pond

Contoocook R.

Contoocook R.

136
47
136
31
31
136
47
137
202
123

The Greenfield Meeting House rests at this corner with its stained glass windows and bell tower. The bells play hymns at noon.

5.3 **At Y, stay straight toward Hancock (Forest Road, unmarked).**
At 5.5 miles on the right is the Greenfield State Park entrance. At 8.0 miles is a covered bridge over the Contoocook River.

9.2 **At stop sign/red blinker cross Route 202. Follow signs toward Hancock.**

10.3 **At stop sign, go straight on Route 123N.**

10.9 **At stop sign in Hancock, bear left, then take an immediate right on Route 137N.**
At this corner is the Hancock Historical Society— a handsome four-chimneyed brick structure.

11.9 **At Y, bear right—follow arrows—still on Route 137N.**
You'll soon see glimpses of Crotched Mountain.

13.9 **At stop sign, left on Route 202E. Soon you'll see a large pond on right.**

15.0 **Turn right on Route 47S in Bennington. Caution: Railroad tracks shortly after this turn!**

15.3 **Stop sign in Bennington center. Go straight on 47S.**
The Bennington Town Hall, near this corner, was built in 1871. It has a slate roof, a spread-winged eagle weather vane, and an ornate cupola. Also here is the Bennington Congregational Church. Built in 1839, it has a double entrance and a clock tower. A large Civil War Minute Man statue also stands at this corner.

Along this road are several great views of Crotched Mountain. You begin a gradual uphill to Francestown.

22.5 **Back at Francestown Village Store.**

5 WILTON–LYNDEBORO

17.4 miles
Challenging, lots of hills. Beginning
around the eight-mile point, it's mostly
uphill for the rest of the trip.

G rab your 35mm camera, a roll of film, and your favorite lens. This tour deserves it! This ride's scenery would even excite Ansel Adams. Maybe your photography skills won't compare to his, but the picture postcard material on this ride will make you look good—even if your shutter experience is limited to instamatics.

The tour encompasses all of the New England clichés. Dignified old churches. Dilapidated red barns. White-fenced paddocks. Farm houses with wrap-around porches. Fragrant apple orchards. Intriguing old cemeteries. And moss-covered stone walls.

Though the beauty of New England is inescapable on this ride, there's another aspect of New England—its historical roots—that is equally noteworthy. Wilton and Lyndeboro were settled in the early 1700s. Though small and rural, these communities understood the importance of intellectual pursuit and cultural enrichment.

When the Transcendental movement was in full swing in the Concord, Massachusetts area in the mid-1800s and notables like Thoreau, Emerson, Dickinson, Melville, and Fuller were making their marks, and lyceums (public lectures) were the rage, Lyndeboro joined ranks and formed

Wilton-
Lyndeboro

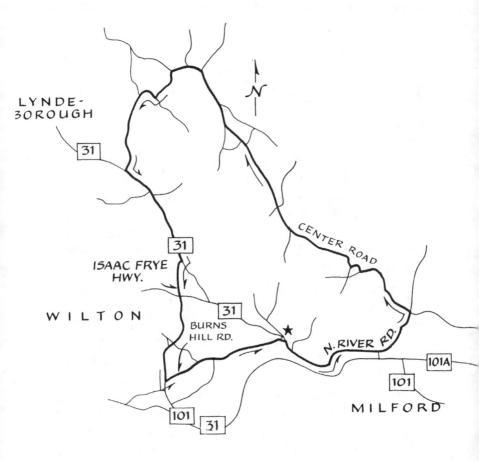

the South Lyndeboro Lyceum. Meeting in a large room over a country store, the weekly gatherings varied from debates by male members to compositions and essays by women. Always well-attended, the meetings provided an opportunity to discuss current political and social issues and ultimately, enrich the community-at-large.

Though most of the history lives on only in town history books, strong visual reminders of colonial roots still exist. You'll cycle past the Lyndeboro Congregational Church built in 1741 and positioned on a hill with a panoramic view of rolling hills beyond. A short side trip finds you at Frye's Measure Mill in Wilton, where since 1750, it has graced the edge of Mill Brook. Listed in the National Register of Historic Places in 1982, the mill now offers a working museum with a fine colonial craft gift shop, a "yesterday" room, and a viewing area of the main mill—still water-powered.

This is a beautiful ride—no matter what time of year. In springtime dogwoods and apple trees burst forth in splendid color. If you choose this trip during lilac season (Mid-May to beginning June) you'll smell these fragrant flowers all along the way. September brings tawny autumn leaves and a cool breeze as you climb the hills. This is the quiet essence of New England.

RIDE INFORMATION

Highlights: Scenic tour! Apple orchards, panoramic views, old New England churches, houses and farms, stone walls, and Frye's Measure Mill (a short side trip).

Start: Wilton Railroad Station, or by the fire department, or on-street parking in downtown Wilton.

RIDE DIRECTIONS

0.0   Right out of the Wilton Station parking lot on Main Street (Route 31S).

0.7   **Turn left on North River Road.**

1.8   **At stop sign/T-intersection, turn left—still on North River Road (unmarked).**

2.5   **At stop sign, turn left on Center Road.**
You climb gradual hills for several miles.

This stretch of road features some super photo opportunities—rolling mountain views, stone walls, Lyndeboro's old church with a weather vane, barn with cupola, white-fenced paddocks, old burial grounds, and farm houses with wrap-around porches. In Lyndeboro, you'll notice Federal-style colonial homes—some with double chimneys and fan-light windows.

10.9   **At stop sign, turn left on Route 31S. Caution: At about 11.4 miles—railroad tracks.**
Route 31S has no shoulder and light traffic.

There's a country store after the railroad tracks, should you want a cold drink.

12.8   **Right on Isaac Frye Highway.**
After you turn, you'll encounter a steep hill followed by several gradual hills.

13.4   **At the stop sign, go straight.**

14.2   **Bear left—still on Isaac Frye Highway (unmarked). (A road to the right is marked Davisville Rd.)**
You'll immediately encounter an uphill.

At about 14.4 miles, if you take a hairpin right by a stone wall and sign: "Frye's Measure Mill 2 mls.," it'll lead you to the mill. The mill has a gift shop, antiques, collectibles, hand-forged ironware, period light fixtures and colonial tin-ware reproductions. Call 603 654-6581 for museum and gift shop hours.

14.9   **Left on Burns Hill Road.**
If you continue straight for another half mile

instead of turning left here, you enter Old Wilton Center. It's worth the effort. Located on a hill, the old center offers a panoramic view. In the 1800s the mills made their appearance and consequently the center of town moved where Wilton Center is now.

17.1 **Railroad tracks. Caution. Over bridge and right on Route 31S.**

17.4 **Where you began in downtown Wilton.**

6 MASON

20.1 miles
Hilly, with four long uphills

Not far from busy Route 101, this ride is an unexpected delight. Mason center, a quiet cluster of Georgian and Federal-style homes gathered around a picturesque colonial Congregational Church, is a quiet, welcome retreat from life's busyness. The pastoral setting is completed by a weathered burial ground with a granite slab wall on a rolling hillside adjacent to the church.

Just down the road a piece from this church, you'll spot a historic marker, "Uncle Sam's House." Nearby stands the humble boyhood home of Samuel Wilson (1766–1854), who was generally known as "Uncle Sam." He supplied beef to the army in 1812. The barrels containing the meat bore the brand: "U.S." The transition from U.S. to "Uncle Sam" followed and became the popular nickname for the United States.

Although this ride was designed for its beautiful backroad scenery—grazing horses, weathered graveyards, and interesting colonial buildings—there was another reason. Food.

There are two places along this route (well, one place isn't right on the route, but a short trip away by car) that are worth planning for—Parker's Maple Barn and Pickity Place.

Visit Parker's Maple Barn (603 878-2308) on this ride and

take an informative maple sugar tour. Learn how sugar sap is collected, processed in the old wood-fired evaporators, and finally consumed on sugar snow, pancakes, or in hot drinks. The restaurant is open for lunch and dinner, but is particularly popular for breakfast. Visit their Corn Crib Gift Shop for handcrafts, native American items, and of course, maple syrup. Open weekends at 7 a.m., and 8 a.m. during the week.

Pickity Place is truly unique. The 200-year old home converted to a restaurant, offers a five-course gourmet lunch from a menu with selections made with their home-grown herbs. Since this is a popular destination and there are only a dozen tables, you'll want to make reservations (603 878-1151). Perhaps plan to have lunch and then ride. The day we indulged in their sumptuous fare, the lunch menu included New England veggie dip, butternut soup, bean salad, herbed white bread, and a choice of chicken crescents or mustard cauliflower quiche for an entree, along with beets with sour cream, and lastly, spiced bread pudding. Available for children, is a smaller portion called Grandmother's basket. Pickity Place is open seven days a week, year round.

The cottage at Pickity Place was the model used for Gramma's house by Golden Books for the American version of Little Red Riding Hood. Visit the Big Bad Wolf and Grandmother's bed in the Red Riding Hood Museum. Take a peek around the gift shop, too. Located 2.5 miles off Route 31. Just follow the signs.

RIDE INFORMATION

Highlights: Pickity Place, Parker's Sugar House, a historic marker, picnic areas, antique shops, pretty scenery.

Start: Congregational Church in Mason Center. To get there, take Route 31S in Wilton (off Route 101W just past Monadnock Springs on left—follow sign toward Mason). Then left on

Route 123S for 2.5 miles to Mason Congregational Church on right, or park on street.

RIDE DIRECTIONS

0.0 **Right out of church driveway on Route 123S.**
Enjoy this downhill—there are a lot of climbs to follow.

ଓଓଓ

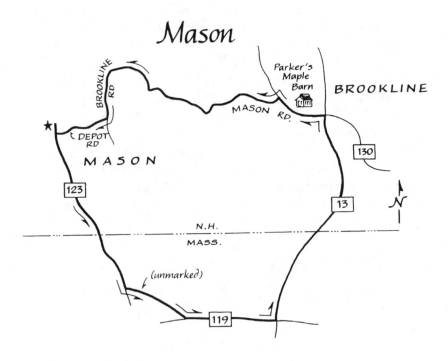

On the right after the church, don't miss the old burying grounds on a rolling hillside with a granite slab wall. At 0.2 mile is a historic marker: Uncle Sam's House.

3.8 **At yield sign, take farthest left (not Old Turnpike Road).**

Soon you cycle over a bridge constructed from granite slabs.

5.2 **At stop sign/T-intersection in Townsend, MA, turn left on Route 119E.**

This is a moderately busy road, no shoulder.

The Old Brick Store is at this turn, should you be in the mood for ice cream. Several attractive brick colonial homes are located at this corner, as well as numerous antique shops.

At about 7.1 miles on the right is the Memorial Hall—an interesting building with stained glass wall plaques honoring men and women who served in the Civil War and WW II.

7.1 **Left on Route 13N. Stay on 13N.**

This road has moderate traffic and a wide shoulder after you cross into New Hampshire.

At this turn is Townsend United Methodist Church, a picturesque New England church with a weathered copper dome. Across the street is the town green where a gazebo and war monument grace the lawn—a nice lunch spot. Townsend has many Federal-style colonial homes with double chimneys.

Along this road are several convenient food marts. You also pass Brookline train station—it's an architecturally interesting structure that is now a residence.

12.9 **At yellow blinker, turn left on Mason Road.**

Potanipo Pond is on the right—a super area for

a picnic.

You'll find Parker's Maple Barn on this road.

16.9   **At Y, bear left on Brookline Road.**
Don't miss the Old Stone Schoolhouse (circa 1790) on this road. It has a 10-foot granite slab base—the same base as the adjacent cemetery wall.

18.4   **Right on Depot Road.** Downhill!

19.4   **At stop sign, turn right on Route 123N (Valley Road).** Uphill.

20.1   **Back at the church.**

MERRIMACK VALLEY REGION

7 HENNIKER– BRADFORD

33.2 miles
Rolling, with many difficult hills

O f the three rides to choose from which begin in Henniker, this is the most scenic. And the most soothing to the spirit—a pause in the middle of life's madness to reacquaint you with nature. There are a number of challenging hills—but consider it a mini-lesson in life—you have to keep climbing the hills and moving beyond where you are. Otherwise no growth occurs. And as in real life, you occasionally encounter the downhills. You've earned them because you've worked hard on the uphills!

This tour begins in Henniker, the only town by its name on Earth, and home of picturesque New England College. The sprawling campus is tucked into the rolling hills of this small New England town—complete with a photogenic covered bridge near the center of town where you begin the tour.

The ride then takes off into the country and presents terrific photo opportunities—cattle and horses grazing in verdant fields, large ponds, old maple trees casting shade on rustic stone walls, panoramic mountain views, colonial white clapboard structures—you know, typical New England stuff. It just doesn't come any better than this, folks!

RIDE INFORMATION

Highlights: New England College, New England scenery—beautiful farms, Contoocook River, a swimming hole, a historic marker, grazing horses and cows, stone walls, mammoth maples, and panoramic views of mountains, fields and trees. A true photo opportunity.

Lodging: You might plan to spend a day or two here. If so, consider staying at a bed and breakfast inn in the area. See Henniker-Hillsboro ride information or check out a New England bed and breakfast book for suggestions.

Start: Center of Henniker, public parking is available near the Henniker Pharmacy or park in a church parking lot. Begin tour at the Western Avenue/Main Street intersection in the center of town by Henniker Pharmacy.

RIDE DIRECTIONS

0.0 **Begin at Henniker Center by the Henniker Pharmacy at Western Avenue/Main Street intersection. Head west toward the school and library (brick buildings) on Western Avenue.**

1.3 **Bear left at Y, still on Western Avenue.**
The calming burble of the Contoocook River will be on your right.

5.0 **At stop sign, turn left on Route 202/9 to Hillsboro. Caution: fast traffic, no breakdown lane.**

6.6 **At stop light by barber shop, go right on School Street. (Becomes Center Road.)**
Ornate Victorian homes line this street, proudly displaying their towers, turrets, gingerbread trim, and wrap-around porches.

As you travel farther on this road, you'll find it to be breathtaking—typical old New England. Beautiful farms, grazing horses and cows, stone walls, and mammoth maples present inspired photo opportunities. After Intrepid Farms, at about 8.4 miles, glance to your right over the stone wall for a panoramic view.

9.7   **Bear right at fork—still on Center Road.**

9.9   **At Y, stay left. (Road becomes East Washington Rd.)**
At about the 10-mile point, there's a historic

೮೮೮೮

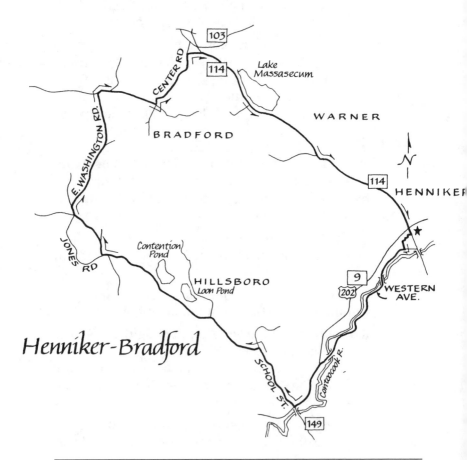

Henniker-Bradford

marker on the right—"Colonial Grant." In 1769, Colonel John Hill granted a tract of land to the first settled minister, the Reverend Jonathan Barnes. The land was to be used for the church, meetinghouse, minister's home, school, pound, training field, and cemetery. Descendants of Reverend Barnes still occupy many of these 18th and early 19th century homes. The minimalist white colonial church, stone wall, birches, and the old cemetery on the hill still grace the quiet grounds today.

It's about this point in the tour that you may begin to resent traffic for intruding on your solitude.

14.2   Right on paved road—not straight on Sleeper Road (gravel).

15.8   With a pond in front of you, bear right on Purling Beck Road. Soon at a fork, go straight on Bradford Spring Road. (Keep the white colonial grange building with cupola on your left.)

The pond at 15.8 miles is a perfect place for a picnic lunch or a refreshing swim.

Soon you'll encounter a mile of hard-packed gravel.

19.9   At stop sign/T, go right on West Road.

21.8   At stop sign, turn left on Center Road.

23.8   Right after yield sign and over narrow bridge.

24.3   Right on Route 114. Wide shoulder.

After turn, on left is Bradford Junction Restaurant and Bakery for a refueling stop.

You'll soon see glimpses of Lake Massasecum on left.

At the 26.8-mile point, Mountain Lake Inn is on your right and a nice view of Lake Massasecum.

33.2   Back at the center of Henniker.

8 HENNIKER–HILLSBORO

11.7 miles
Challenging, lots of long hills

O ne of the virtues of the Henniker rides (choose from three—they all start at the same place) is that they lack commercial overexposure. You can pedal unhurriedly along byways and discover historic covered bridges, long stretches of rolling pastures, and refreshing ponds. Small villages along the way preserve an unspoken devotion to quietude. The serene country roads twist and wind to open up new scenes around every bend.

This tour begins in Henniker, the only town with this name on earth, and home of picturesque New England College. The sprawling campus is tucked among the rolling hills of this small New England village—complete with a photo-opportunity covered bridge near the center of town where the tour begins.

The shortest of the three Henniker tours, this ride loops through Hillsboro. A wonderfully well-preserved historic town, Hillsboro is also the location of the Franklin Pierce Homestead. Built in 1804 by Benjamin Pierce, a general in the American Revolution and father of Franklin Pierce, the fourteenth president of the United States, the homestead was designated a National Historic Landmark in 1961. You may want to plan a side trip to tour the Pierce Homestead.

Though short, this ride can be quite challenging. Don't forget it's OK to walk your bike. Enjoy it!

RIDE INFORMATION

Highlights: New England College and a pretty ride along the Contoocook River.

Lodging: If you'd like to make a weekend of this tour, consider staying at the Colby Hill Inn (603 428-3281) in Henniker, a lovely Federal home that leans a bit here and there, which only adds to its charm. Or try The Meeting House (603 428-3228), where you can also indulge in some whitewater activities on the Contoocook River, or enjoy summer theater in nearby towns. Another consideration for overnight accommodations is the Inn at Maplewood Farm in Hillsboro. (603 464-4242), a 1794 farm house in a pastoral country setting.

Start: In the center of Henniker, public parking is available near the Henniker Pharmacy or park in a church parking lot. Begin tour at the Western Avenue/Main Street intersection in the center of town by Henniker Pharmacy.

RIDE DIRECTIONS

0.0 From the Main Street/Western Avenue intersection, head west on Western Avenue toward the school and library (brick buildings).
At 0.5 mile is the Colby Hill Inn.

1.3 At Y intersection, go left—still on Western Avenue.
As you wind your way along this road, the burbling Contoocook River will be on your right.

5.0 At stop sign, turn left on Route 202/9W. Caution: Fast traffic. No shoulder.

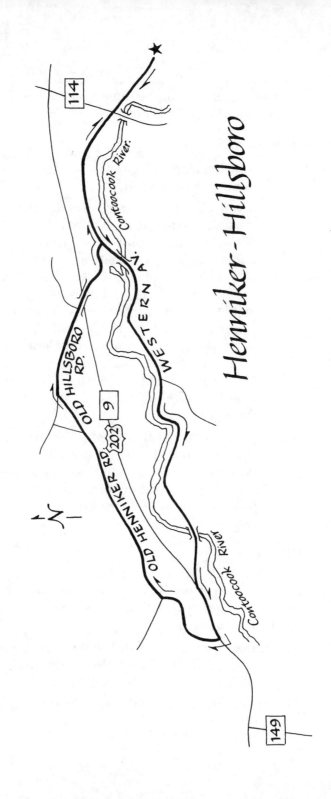

Henniker-Hillsboro

Soon you enter Hillsboro. There are numerous places in town to eat.

5.7   Make a hairpin right turn on to Old Henniker Road (unmarked) by a mobile home park. Agway is on your left just before this turn.

6.4   At Y, by large boulder, bear right on Old Hillsboro Road.
You'll soon cycle past a couple of attractive, double-chimneyed colonial homes.

10.3   At stop sign, go left. You're back on Western Avenue.

11.7   You're back at intersection at center of Henniker where ride began.
Stop in at the Henniker Pharmacy if you're in need of refreshments. They have one of the best selections of sparkling waters to be found. A grill is also available for a sandwich or burger.

9 HENNIKER– HOPKINTON

17.9 miles
Challenging, two long, steep hills

This is a short ride—only 17.9 miles. It's the perfect stress reliever. Nature soothes the soul as nothing else can. To experience the solitude and beauty of nature puts us in better touch with our inner world.

In addition to the visual beauty of this ride, there's the healing power of the *sound* of nature. The Contoocook River burbles and chortles as you pedal along beside it. The sound is rejuvenating! You can't help but enjoy this ride.

Beginning in Henniker, the ride then continues on to Hopkinton, a small town that entered the present era while retaining a distinctive colonial character. In colonial days, good soil and plentiful water created a favorable environment for prosperous farmers and millers who built substantial homes here. Later, when the town served as a county seat, it attracted people of means. Its proximity to Concord drew state government officials, professional people, and others who appreciated the 18th century atmosphere.

This is a pretty ride—one of three Henniker rides. You may want to make a weekend of it, stay at a local inn and do all three rides! Much of this tour follows the Contoocook River. It can be challenging at times—but what are you doing this for anyway? To get exercise and see the backroads of southern New Hampshire, right? Then you'll love it!

RIDE INFORMATION

Highlights: New England College, two covered bridges, the Fiber Studio, Elm Brook Park Recreation Area, French Pond (a public swimming beach), Hopkinton Dam, and the Hopkinton-Everett Reservoir, numerous craft shops, Pat's Peak, and a scenic ride along the Contoocook River.

Lodging: If you decide to do two or three of the Henniker rides, consider staying at a bed and breakfast inn in the area. See Henniker-Hillsboro ride information or check out a New England bed and breakfast book for suggestions.

Start: In the center of Henniker, public parking is available near the Henniker Pharmacy, or park in a church parking lot. Begin tour from the Western Avenue/Main Street intersection in the center of town by Henniker Pharmacy.

RIDE DIRECTIONS

0.0 **From the Main Street/Western Avenue intersection, head west on Western Avenue toward the school and library (brick buildings).**

0.5 **Right on Route 202/9E. This road has fast traffic, but offers a wide shoulder.**

1.4 **Left on Foster Hill Road.**

You begin a long, arduous climb as you turn on this road. At about 1.7 miles is the Fiber Studio. If you're interested in knitting, dyeing, spinning or weaving, it's worth a stop.

At about 2.0 miles you begin the most difficult

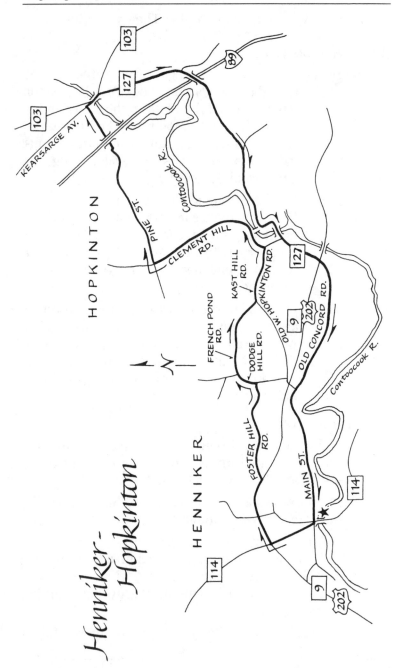

Henniker-
Hopkinton

hill on the tour—it's only 0.4 of a mile long, but you'll know you're climbing. Hang in—it's downhill on the other side! But take it slow on the downhill—it's bumpy.

2.8　**At stop sign/T, turn left on Dodge Hill Road.**

3.0　**Bear right on French Pond Road.**
On your right watch for French Pond at 3.6 miles. It's a public swimming beach.

4.2　**At stop sign/T, left on Kast Hill Road.**
This is a bumpy road.

4.9　**At Y, turn left on Clement Hill Road (unmarked).**
Don't miss the covered bridge on your right at about 5.2 miles.

5.4　**Bear left with curve (stay on pavement).**

6.7　**At stop sign, turn right on Pine Street (unmarked).**

9.0　**At stop sign, turn right on Kearsarge Street as you enter Hopkinton.**
If you glance to your left at about the 11 o'clock position shortly after making this turn, you'll see another covered bridge.

9.1　**Bear right on Route 127S (Mr. Mike's will be to your left).**
This road has no shoulder, but little traffic.

Soon the Contoocook River meanders along on your right.

At about 11.8 miles, Elm Brook Park Recreation Area welcomes you to stop and have a picnic lunch.

At 13.2 miles is the Hopkinton Dam and the Hopkinton-Everett Reservoir.

13.4　**At T, turn left (still on Route 127S).**

14.1　**At stop sign at Route 202/9 intersection, cross the road to Old Concord Road.**

At this intersection, The Golden Pineapple boasts over 2,500 square feet of showroom, displaying New England pottery, linens, a tempting selection of gourmet foods and kitchen gadgets, jewelry, glassware, and other collectibles.

16.1   At stop sign (with gas station on your left), continue straight on Main Street (unmarked). It takes you back to Henniker center.

If you glance left on this road, you'll see Pat's Peak, a popular ski area. Also along this road is a U-Pick Strawberry Patch. If your timing is right and the berries are ripe, you can pick a quart of these succulent berries and dump them over frozen strawberry yogurt tonight!

17.9   You're back at the beginning of your trip.

If you want to grab a bite to eat, there are a variety of places to choose from. Check out Main Street Pizza which, in addition to pizzas, also has super grinders. Or try Henniker Pharmacy. They have a small sit-down sandwich counter. Daniel's Restaurant overlooking the river is a wonderful lunch stop—great soups and sandwiches.

10 WARNER–SALISBURY

10.4, 13.9, 24.3, 33.7 or 42.3 miles
Hilly, long climbs, a 2.7-mile stretch of
gravel, extension rides—very challenging

I f you're awed by New England foliage, consider choosing this tour during Columbus Day weekend in October. Not only will you be treated to some of the most spectacular foliage in New England, but you'll be in town for the biggest event of the year in Warner—the Fall Foliage Festival. The only catch is, you'll have to contend with people—lots of them. The festival typically draws thousands to watch the oxen-pulling and tree-felling contests, check out the midway, observe the pottery and basket-weaving demonstrations, and of course, indulge in the baked goods and hot, spiced cider!

Warner, 20 miles northwest of Concord, lies in the rolling foothills of the Contoocook River Valley between Mount Kearsarge and Mount Sunapee. It's a haven for artists—painters, sculptors, writers. One reason is that Warner is near Concord where the League of New Hampshire Craftsmen is headquartered. Many artists market their work through the League.

Warner is also home to a number of historic buildings— double-chimneyed, Federal-style colonial residences with fan-light windows over entry doors, an old, colonial meeting house and the Pillsbury Library, which opened in 1891. The library was a gift from George A. Pillsbury, who earned his fortune from the flour-mill industry.

Also of note is the Mt. Kearsarge Indian Museum. Former curator of the Canterbury Shaker Village for 30 years, Bud Thompson, has amassed one of the finest Native American artifacts collections of its kind in New England. The facility, also home to a theater and museum shop, is open Monday-Saturday from 10-5 and Sunday from noon-5 p.m., May through October and on weekends after that through Christmas. Tours are available. An admission fee is charged.

You choose the level of challenge you want on this ride—moderately challenging (24.3 miles), or add on the Mt. Kearsarge ranger station extension (total: 33.7 miles), or very challenging (42.3 miles) with the summit extension. Or skip the 24.3 ride and just do the ranger station (10.4 miles) or continue to the summit (13.9 miles).

RIDE INFORMATION

Highlights: Spectacular mountain views, buffalo farm, Kearsarge Indian Museum, Mount Kearsarge, hiking, and picnic area.

Start: Warner Post Office parking lot. To get there, take I-89N to exit 8. Go left off exit toward Warner on Route 103W for 1.4 miles. The post office is on the left.

RIDE DIRECTIONS

(First loop: 24.3-miles)

0.0   From the post office parking lot, cross the street, go right on School Street by the fire station.

0.3   At Y, left on Pumpkin Hill Road.

2.0   Follow arrow signs toward right— still on Pumpkin Hill Road—not straight on gravel. (Pumpkin Hill Road soon becomes Warner Road.)

A buffalo farm is nestled in the valley on the right at about 2.5 miles.

Near the 6-mile point you'll encounter hard-packed gravel for 2.7 miles. You may want to walk your bike.

6.1   At four-way intersection, go straight on Warner Road.

9.3   At stop sign, turn right on Route 127S, where traffic is fast, but infrequent.

19.0   At stop sign, turn right on Route 103W—it also has fast, infrequent traffic.
A country store is at this corner.

24.3   Left into post office parking lot.

RIDE DIRECTIONS:

(Short extension—10.4 alone or 33.7 miles when combined with initial loop).

This ride adds the Mount Kearsarge ranger station extension to the first loop above (24.3 miles), which makes it a 33.7-mile ride. (Or 10.4 miles if you skip the 24.3-mile loop.) You'll end at the ranger's station, where there are picnic tables.

0.0   Left out of post office parking lot on Route 103W.

0.2   Right on Kearsarge Street—it's the left side of the Y—to the left of the monument.
At 1.2 miles on right is the Mt. Kearsarge Indian Museum.

5.2   You've arrived at the ranger station of Rollins Park on Mount Kearsarge. Turn around and retrace the route back to the post office.

10.4   Back at the post office.

RIDE DIRECTIONS:

(Long extension—13.9 or 42.3 miles when combined with initial loop).

This ride continues on from the one preceding to the

Warner-Salisbury

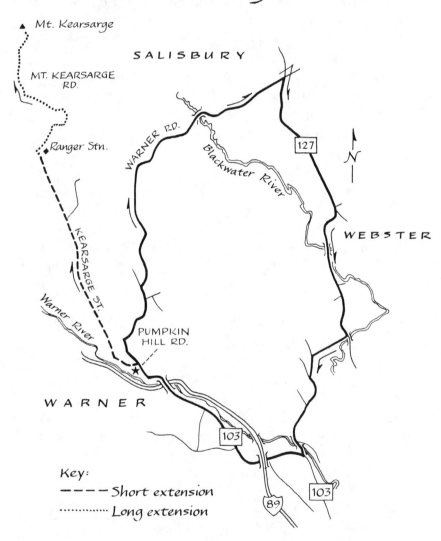

Mt. Kearsarge

MT. KEARSARGE RD.

SALISBURY

Ranger Stn.

WARNER RD.

Blackwater River

127

N

KEARSARGE ST.

WEBSTER

Warner River

PUMPKIN HILL RD.

WARNER

103

103

89

Key:
— — — Short extension
.... Long extension

Mount Kearsarge summit. If you do it in addition to the first loop (24.3 miles), it's a 42.3-mile ride. Or skip the 24.3-mile loop and ride directly to the summit for a 13.9-mile ride. This is *not* for the unseasoned cyclist. You must have immense stamina to climb this mountain. But it can be done!

Follow directions for the ride immediately above, except continue to the summit—another 3.5 miles. Once there, you can hike another half mile to the top of Mount Kearsarge. A gorgeous view awaits you—one of the best in the state. To the west is Mount Ascutney in Vermont, to the south is Mount Monadnock, and to the north Cardigan, White Face, and Chocorua Mountains stand against the horizon. Picnic tables here offer a much-deserved reward for having climbed the mountain on a bike!

Retrace the route back to the post office. Combined with the first loop, total mileage will be 42.3.

11 NEW BOSTON-GREENFIELD

40+/- or 50.9 miles
Rolling, many hills, some steep

Two. Two. Two rides in one. No matter if you choose to ride the short (!) 40-miler or the longer 51-mile ride, you will not be disappointed. Lots of farms, scenic vistas, country stores, and New Hampshire cycling at its best.

New Boston's town square, where the rides begin, burned down in 1880. When it was rebuilt, the buildings were predictably Victorian. It's a quintessential New England town square with Dodge's Store, a classic white New England church, and even the Molly Stark Cannon. The historic cannon is housed in a small building on the common.

If your timing is right you may cycle through this area when New Boston hosts the Hillsborough County Agricultural Fair in early September, or the New Hampshire Sheep and Wool Festival on Mother's Day weekend.

Traveling west to Francestown, Bennington, and then Greenfield, you will experience some of NH's most breathtaking foliage, if you're riding in the fall. In Greenfield, a short cut can take you back to New Boston, or if you're up for a challenge, continue south to Lyndeborough and Mont Vernon.

From Mont Vernon the route continues south through

a corner of Milford, where you might catch a glimpse of the Hot Air Balloon Show at the end of June. Milford, long known as the Granite Town of the Granite State because of its voluminous quarrying of granite, is also the proud owner of one of the oldest Paul Revere bells. It tolls faithfully in the belfry of the Town House clock tower every hour.

Traveling on to Amherst, a gracious, historic New England town, you may want to stop by the library for a walking-tour pamphlet. The town common is surrounded by fine examples of Palladian architecture, Greek revival doorways, colonial and Victorian architecture and, of course, Federal-style homes.

RIDE INFORMATION

Highlights: A quiet, scenic ride, in a classic New England setting. Historic markers. Stone walls, old burying grounds. A wonderful old country store or two. And some hills to give you a good workout.

Start: New Boston parking lot across from the fire station.

RIDE DIRECTIONS

0.0 **Right out of the parking lot on Meeting House Hill Road toward the country store and the bridge. Meeting Hill Road goes onto Rte. 13.**
Dodge's Store, an old-fashioned country store, complete with worn, squeaky floor boards, is in the town square.

0.1 **At stop sign, right on Rte. 136/77.**

0.4 **Bear left to stay on Rte. 136.**
A couple of historic markers are located along this road after the 7-mile mark.

7.8 **Right turn into Francestown onto Rte. 47N.**
At this corner is the Old Meeting House of

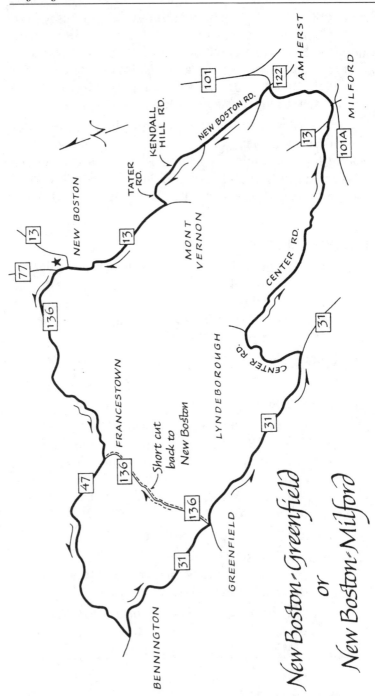

101

122 AMHERST

MILFORD

NEW BOSTON RD.

KENDALL HILL RD.

13

101A MILFORD

TATER RD.

13

NEW BOSTON

13

MONT VERNON

CENTER RD.

136

31

77

★

CENTER RD.

FRANCESTOWN

LYNDEBOROUGH

47

136

Short cut back to New Boston

136

31

GREENFIELD

31

BENNINGTON

New Boston-Greenfield
or
New Boston-Milford

Francestown, built in 1801. It features classic New England design—dentil molding, black shutters, columned facade, and a steeple.

Also another country store after this turn.

15.0 At stop sign, left on Rte. 31S in Bennington.

At this turn, there's a restaurant and country store. If you take a right turn you can go visit the Bennington Historic Museum.

20.2 At stop sign in Greenfield, go left to stay on Rte 31S.

Country store on right.

***

If you want a shorter ride (40+/- miles), turn left here onto Rte. 136 which takes you back to New Boston.

***

27.0 Left on Center Road. Sign says, "Lyndeboro Center." A bit hilly with some steep downhills. Be careful on the descents because some sharp corners are mixed in.

At the crest of your climb in Lyndeboro by the colonial church, fabulous panoramic views unfold in the distance. Especially pretty in the fall.

34.1 Continue straight on Center Road toward Milford.

At the 36-mile point, consider a stop at the Milford Fish Hatchery, open 8 a.m. to 4 p.m.

37.9 At stop sign, bear right on Rte. 13S.

38.3 Straight at stop sign toward 101E and Amherst.

38.4 Straight at stop sign on what is Amherst St. (unmarked). (Sign on your left says Grove St.)

40.6 Left by sign that says "Amherst Village Green."

40.8 Left at the flag pole onto Boston Post Road.
Country store on the right.

41.2 Bear right by school on New Boston Road (un-

marked).

42.1 **Continue straight on New Boston Road. (Road becomes Brook Road, then Kendall Hill Road.)**

43.4 **Bear right on Kendall Hill Road—becomes Tater Road.**

At this intersection, you can take a left on Brook Road, and visit Beaver Brook Farm Museum.

Prepare for lots of uphills on this stretch.

46.6 **At stop sign, right on Rte. 13 (unmarked).**

50.8 **Right to stay on Rte. 13.**

50.9 **Left into parking lot.**

12 PEMBROKE– CHICHESTER

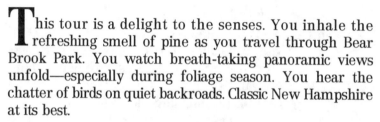

29 miles
Rolling with several long,
steady uphill climbs

This tour is a delight to the senses. You inhale the refreshing smell of pine as you travel through Bear Brook Park. You watch breath-taking panoramic views unfold—especially during foliage season. You hear the chatter of birds on quiet backroads. Classic New Hampshire at its best.

The ride begins in Pembroke, a bedroom community for Manchester and Concord. The ride leaves from Pembroke Fire Station—which is usually deserted—except in early July when there's a statewide fire fighter's muster. So depending on your sense of adventure, either avoid or choose this ride during that time of year. (For exact date of the muster, check with the Pembroke Fire Department.)

Pembroke's contribution to New England charm is its understatement. It offers simple colonial churches and buildings, rambling Victorian homes, and a park dedicated to those who fought in wars to defend our country.

Soon you find yourself in out-of-the-way and lost-in-time Chichester. An unexpected jewel, this little village has a classic colonial Methodist church with intricate stained glass windows and Gothic arches.

But the best part of the ride is the scenery. You travel through Bear Brook State Park—9,300 acres of wilderness. You pedal hard up a long incline and as you crest the hill, a picture-perfect scene greets you—cattle grazing in distant fields and a simple colonial church beside a comfortable old farmhouse with large maples. You cruise past numerous panoramic views that are worth a stop—and a picture! This is after all, New Hampshire!

RIDE INFORMATION

Highlights: Swimming in Bear Brook Park, gorgeous scenery, historic colonial buildings, historic marker, Bear Brook Snowmobile Museum, Steeplegate Mall.

Start: At Pembroke Fire Station on Route 3. If you're heading north, it's on the right just after the first set of lights. Fire department officials ask that cars be parked toward the rear on the building's left side.

RIDE DIRECTIONS

0.0 **Right out of fire station on Route 3N.**

A busy road with fast traffic, but with a wide shoulder.

Soon on your right the First Congregational Church appears, a simple, white clapboard structure established in 1733. At 1.1 miles a historic marker on the left records the site of the First Church and Meetinghouse. Also along this road are attractive brick colonials and turreted, white Victorian homes.

2.9 **Right on Route 106N.**

Be careful—this road has lots of traffic, but also a wide shoulder. At 6.0 miles, turn left if you want to visit the Steeplegate Mall.

8.9 **Right on Staniels Road.**

At 9.0 miles there's a one-lane wooden bridge over the Suncook River. It's a pretty place for a rest stop. This is a lovely road with working farms and white picket fences.

9.7 **Turn left on Ricker Road.**

10.3 **At stop sign, turn right, then take an immediate left on Canterbury Road.**
This is a pretty road. Shaded by mammoth sugar maples flanking stone walls, you pedal past stately colonial farmhouses with attached barns.

12.5 **At stop sign, continue straight on Main Street (unmarked) in Chichester.**
A classic New England church, Chichester Methodist Church, graces the town center with its Gothic spires, arches, and intricate stained glass windows.

13.1 **Bear left on pavement—not straight on gravel.**
At 13.3 miles there's a gorgeous panoramic vista on right—especially if you're riding in the fall. Immediately after this view is a small, colonial Gothic church—Chichester Congregational Church. With its Gothic-arched shutters, stained glass windows, and a cupola with weather vane, it looks like a twin sister of the Methodist church.

This road has beautiful, well-kept properties—wonderful old barns, white rail fences, meticulously cut lawns, and working farms with Holstein cattle grazing lazily in the pastures.

14.6 **At stop sign/T at Route 28, go left a very short way, then right on Depot Road.**

17.3 **At light in Epsom, left on Route 202 (unmarked).**
Gossville General Store is on your right at this corner, and then Copper Horse Antiques, should you want to go treasure hunting.

17.6 **Right on Black Hall Road.**

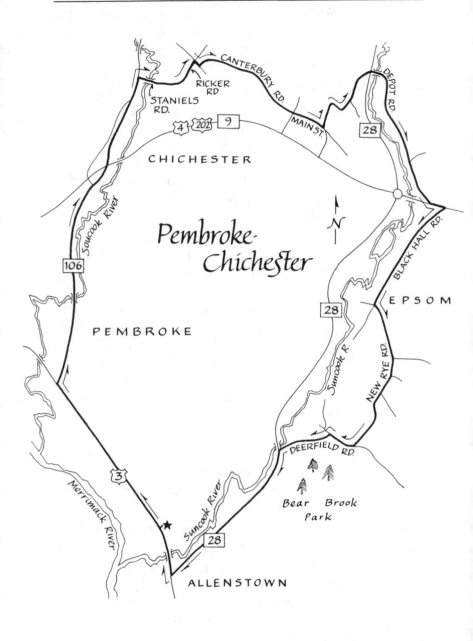

19.9 **At four-way stop sign, go left on New Rye Road. (The street sign is to your left.)**

You'll encounter a long climb, but persevere— the scene at the top is worth it. A simple colonial church resides near a comfortable old farmhouse with large maples gracing the yard. Cattle and horses munch on grass in distant fields as a magnificent panoramic view unfolds on the right.

At about 22.6 miles you'll notice lots of evergreen trees and the refreshing smell of pine. You're now in Bear Brook State Park.

22.9 **At stop sign/T, go right on Deerfield Road (unmarked).**

At 23.4 miles in Bear Brook State Park, on the right, public picnic tables and swimming are available. The park also offers a snowmobile museum, nature center, fitness course, boat rentals, fishing, and camping. Make a day of it!

On this road a historic building, the Old Allenstown Meeting House, circa 1815, resides.

24.5 **At stop sign, turn left on Route 28S.**

Route 28 has heavy traffic, but a wide shoulder.

The Suncook River Convenience Store is at 25.0 miles.

27.6 **At stop sign, go right on Route 3N.**

At 28.8 miles is Pembroke Park, home to war memorial cannons, an artillery gun, and a statue honoring WWI, WWII, Korean, and Vietnam veterans.

29.0 **The Pembroke Fire Station is on the right.**

13 BOW–DUNBARTON

27.6 miles
Challenging, hilly,
several long climbs

A s you cycle past cozy cottages with stone walls overgrown with ivy and tiger lilies, past horses munching
on hay in white-fenced paddocks, and past fragrant fields of
newly mown alfalfa, it's difficult to believe you're so near
bustling Routes I-93 and I-89.

The town of Bow, incorporated in 1727, is considered a
bedroom community for state capital Concord. It is located
on the banks of the Merrimack River.

Near the halfway point in this ride, you'll enter the
frozen-in-time village of Dunbarton. Incorporated in 1765,
it was named for Dunbartonshire, Scotland, site of the
famous Dunbar Castle.

The historic Stark House in Dunbarton is on this tour. A
New Hampshire landmark, the Federal-style building with
its black shutters and three mammoth maple trees on the
front lawn was built by Molly Stark's father, Captain Caleb
Page, circa 1759. This was Molly Page's home in her youth
and later as the wife of General John Stark. In 1834, the
structure housed the first Dunbarton Post Office and still
contains original stencilling by artist Moses Eaton. Stark
House is a private home and not open to the public.

Consider a trip to nearby Concord—home of the Christa
McAuliffe Planetarium, the well-known Concord Coaches,

New Hampshire Historical Society, the 1819 State House, and the Audubon Society of New Hampshire.

Just off the beaten path, the Bow-Dunbarton tour is a nice ride, but challenging. You begin with a long, uphill climb and end with several moderate hills. You may want to make a day of it. Perhaps bring a lunch and take your time and just enjoy the beauty of New Hampshire backroads.

RIDE INFORMATION

Highlights: Bow Town Hall, Bow Historical Center, Black Brook, Clough State Park and Everett Dam, colonial Dunbarton center and historic Molly Stark House, Audubon Society of New Hampshire.

Start: In Concord, take I-89N to the Bow exit—which is immediately after you get on I-89 from I-93. At the stop sign at the end of the exit by the gas station, turn right on Logging Hill Road. Go 2.8 miles. On the left is a white colonial structure with black shutters—Bow Town Hall built in 1847. Park here.

RIDE DIRECTIONS

0.0 **Left out of Bow Town Hall parking lot.**
This is a beautiful, tree-lined road with little traffic.

You soon encounter a mile-long uphill climb. It's worth it—at the crest, look off to your left—a panoramic view unfolds.

7.7 **Right on Black Brook Road.**

12.1 **Straight on Black Brook Road. Don't bear right on Long Pond Road.**
Black Brook Road is an attractive road that snakes along Black Brook.

13.3 **At stop sign/T, go left—still on Black Brook Road (unmarked). This T intersection is surrounded by**

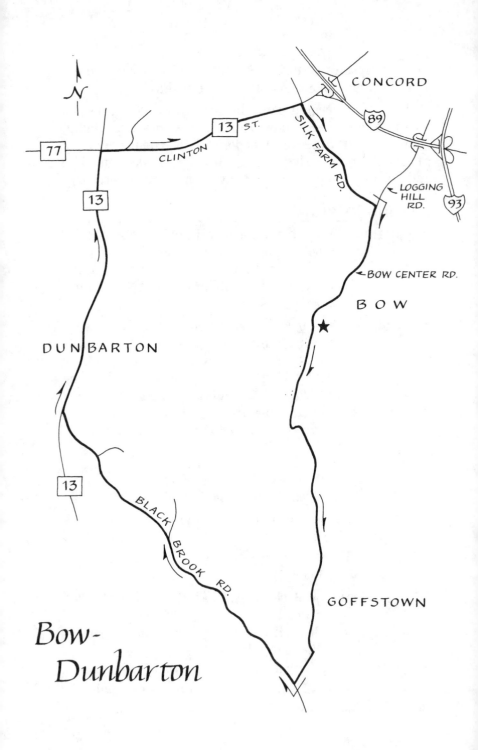

CONCORD

89

13 ST.

77

CLINTON

SILK FARM RD.

13

LOGGING
HILL
RD.

93

BOW CENTER RD.

BOW

★

DUNBARTON

13

BLACK BROOK RD.

GOFFSTOWN

*Bow-
Dunbarton*

trees and has a large boulder and brook on the left.

14.2 **At stop sign, turn right on Route 13N (unmarked).**
There's a large birch tree on right at this corner.
This road has fast, but light traffic. No shoulder.
There is one long uphill climb, followed by an
invigorating descent a few miles later.

You'll soon find yourself in the quiet New England village of Dunbarton. Fronting the green
are elegant white houses with dark shutters,
white picket fences, and large porches. The town
hall features unusual architecture in that it has
two porticos. The Congregational church across
the street, founded in 1769, is elaborate for its
time. Black, Gothic-arched shutters create a stark
contrast against the pristine white clapboard
structure, which is capped with a gold dome.

At about the 16.7-mile mark on the left is the
Dunbarton Town Pound built in 1791.

At 18.6 miles, a country store is on the left—great
stop for juice, ice cream, sodas. They also have a
deli. This corner is also the left turn to Clough
State Park, where you can swim and picnic.

At 19.5 miles on the left is the historic Stark House.

19.5 **At stop sign/blinking yellow light, turn right on**
Route 13N.
This road has heavy traffic and no shoulder.

23.3 **At yellow blinker, turn right on Silk Farm Road.**
To visit the Audubon Center, take a left on Silk
Farm Road. It's a half mile down on your left. The
New Hampshire Audubon Society headquarters
has a gift shop, nature center, and bird aviary.

25.5 **At stop sign, turn right on Logging Hill Road.**
There are numerous hills on this road.

27.6 **Town Hall is on the left.**

14 HOOKSETT–BOW

34.8 miles
Challenging, very hilly. Several long,
tough hills. Two miles of gravel road.

I f traveling easy country lanes past active farms, grazing
cows and horses, sparkling clear ponds, rumbling rivers,
and charming New England colonial homes, sounds exhilarating, this tour is for you. There's even an element of
ruggedness thrown in—you encounter two miles of gravel
with some loose rocks and sand. It's manageable—even ideal
for a cross bike or a mountain bike. But you'll do just fine
on a touring bike also—although you may want to walk that
short way. It's a pleasant, deserted stretch of road—with a
perfect opportunity to chit-chat.

This ride leads you through a number of small bedroom
communities—Hooksett, Bow, Dunbarton, Goffstown,
through a corner of Manchester, and back to Hooksett.
Because you're so near Manchester, you may want to do
some sight-seeing there.

The Currier Gallery of Art is considered one of the finest
around—with its collection of western European paintings
and sculptures from the 13th through the 20th centuries,
and its American paintings, glass, silver, and pewter from the
18th through 20th centuries. A large collection of furniture
emphasizes New Hampshire-made pieces. (Admission fee is
$4. Call 603 669-6144 for hours.)

Manchester Historical Association is also worth a visit. It showcases the history of the state's largest city. Documents, maps, diaries, old photographs, newspapers, and the archives of the Amoskeag Manufacturing Company can all be found here. Highlighting the museum's collection are firefighting apparatus, Victorian costumes, fine furniture, and belongings of General John Stark. (Tues.–Friday, 9–4, Sat. 10–4. Free. Call 603 622-7531.)

Manchester has its own charm. You'll find the contemporary Center of New Hampshire complex and the new telephone building blend beautifully with the fully restored Palace Theater (built in 1915), or the charming brick row houses built in 1881 along Canal Street to house mill workers.

Most of your time is spent nowhere near the busy Manchester area—but rather, out on the backroads of the surrounding rural towns. It's truly backroads New Hampshire at its best!

RIDE INFORMATION

Highlights: Pleasant country scenery, colonial buildings, skyline view of Manchester.

Start: University of New Hampshire parking lot in Hooksett. Take exit 7 off I-293N in Hooksett for 1.7 miles to Hackett Hill Road. Left on Hackett Hill Road for 0.4 mile, then turn left and park in the UNH parking lot.

RIDE DIRECTIONS

0.0 **At stop sign in UNH parking lot, turn left on Hackett Hill Road, a smooth-surfaced road with little traffic.**
This road climbs awhile, then has a long descent.

4.5 **At stop sign, turn left on Route 3A north.**
This road has fast traffic and no shoulder. You'll be on it for less than a mile. The Merrimack River is on your right.

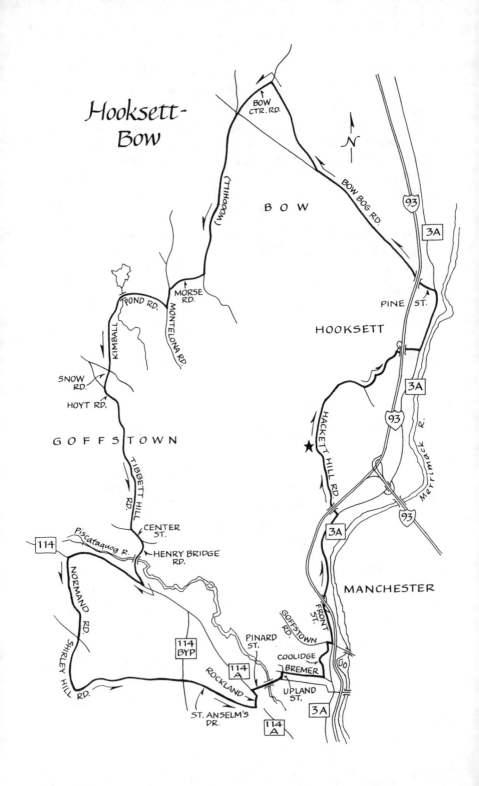

Hooksett-
Bow

BOW CTR. RD.

N

BOW BOG RD.

93

3A

(WOODHILL)

BOW

MORSE
RD.

MONTELONA RD.

POND RD.

KIMBALL

SNOW
RD.

HOYT RD.

PINE ST.

HOOKSETT

3A

93

Merrimack R.

GOFFSTOWN

TIBBETT HILL RD.

HACKETT HILL RD.

★

93

CENTER
ST.

Piscataquog R.

HENRY BRIDGE
RD.

3A

114

NORMAND RD.

SHIRLEY HILL RD.

114
BYP

114
A

PINARD
ST.

ROCKLAND

GOFFSTOWN RD.

FRONT ST.

MANCHESTER

COOLIDGE
BREMER

UPLAND
ST.

3A

ST. ANSELM'S
DR.

114
A

5.4   **Left on Pine Street (becomes Bow Bog Road in Bow), a hilly, tree-lined country road.**
       At 8.1 miles on the right is the colonial Bow Bog Meeting House built in 1835.

10.2   **At T/stop sign, turn left on Bow Center Road (unmarked).**
       Two long, steep uphills await you on this road. Hey—smile—you're doing this for your health!

14.0   **Right on Morse Road.**

14.8   **At stop sign/T-intersection, turn left on Montelona Road.**
       This road is bumpy.

15.0   **Right on Kimball Road (unmarked), a gravel road with loose rocks and sand. A mile in, this road turns to the left.**
       To avoid a possible flat tire, you may want to walk your bike on Kimball Pond Road.

       If you take a right at about the 15.9-mile mark, Kimball Pond is down the paved road a short way. It's a pretty stop for a picnic lunch.

17.4   **At stop sign, go straight on Snow Road (unmarked).**

17.7   **At stop sign/T, bear left on Hoyt Road (unmarked, becomes Tibbett Hill Road).**

20.3   **At stop sign, go left on Center Street (unmarked, there's a tall boulder on left).**

20.7   **Right on Henry Bridge Road.**
       For a refreshment stop or to refill your water bottle, stop here at Grasmere General Store.

21.8   **At stop light, turn right on Route 114N.**
       This road has a wide shoulder and busy traffic. Soon on the left is Magoo's Drive Inn where you can refuel with a BLT, tuna, roast beef, or a seafood sub. Or, if it's a crisp fall day, try hot chocolate!

23.5 **Left on Normand Road by ball parks.**
This is a long, steady uphill climb.

25.0 **At stop sign, continue straight to Shirley Hill Road.**
The word "hill" is in this road's name for a reason—you'll soon find out. But then, there's a looooong downhill coast.

An attractive skyline view of Manchester appears on the left at about 25.3 miles.

28.1 **At stop light, cross to St. Anselm's Drive.**

29.5 **At stop sign, turn left on Rockland Street.**
A block or so up on this street on the right is Bob Nadeau's House of Subs—a definite stop if you're a sub connoisseur.

29.7 **At stop sign, turn left on Mast Road (Route 114A) for 0.1 mile to stop light. This is busy, city traffic.**

29.8 **At stop light, turn right on Pinard Street, cross the bridge into Manchester.**

30.4 **After the bridge, turn left on Upland Street for a block, then right on Bremer Street.**

31.2 **Left on Coolidge Ave.**

32.0 **At this Goffstown Road stop sign, walk your bike across the street. After you reach the other sidewalk, turn right, walk to the corner, cross Front Street (Unmarked. Fast-trafficked I-293 to your right), then left on Front Street.**

32.7 **At stop sign/red blinker, cautiously merge left on Route 3A. Very busy road. Caution: Danger! Shortly after this stop sign, vehicle traffic merges from the right off a major highway.**

34.4 **Left on Hackett Hill Road.**

34.8 **Left into UNH parking lot where you began your ride.**

15 HOOKSETT– DUNBARTON

49.6 miles
Moderately difficult with several long
hills, a mile of packed gravel

Despite its nearness to the state's largest city—Manchester—this ride is surprisingly undaunted by the interruption of traffic or overdevelopment. Instead, you ride past mature birch stands, stone walls, sheep and horses grazing, and, if your timing's right, even a great blue heron fishing in a marsh.

The refreshing scent of pine greets you as you travel through attractive residential areas. And if you revel in the quaintness and sense of solitude of days long since past, you'll exult as you pedal into Dunbarton.

Dunbarton, incorporated in 1765, was named for Dunbartonshire, Scotland, site of the famous Dunbar Castle. Dunbarton, New Hampshire is perhaps less well-known, but nonetheless holds its own in the "classic New England" category. Fronting the green in this quiet village are elegant white clapboard houses with dark shutters, white picket fences, and large porches. The town hall features unusual architecture in that it has two porticos. The Congregational Church (founded in 1769), across the street from the town hall, is elaborate for its time. Black, Gothic-arched shutters create a stark contrast against this church's pristine white clapboards. The structure is capped with a gold dome.

This is a super ride—but for the more seasoned cyclist—due to distance and terrain. It's worth the challenge. Happy cycling!

RIDE INFORMATION

Highlights: A very pretty ride, berry-picking opportunities, historic buildings, quaint and quiet Dunbarton.

Start: University of New Hampshire parking lot in Hooksett. Take exit 7 off I-293N in Hooksett for 1.7 miles to Hackett Hill Road. Left on Hackett Hill Road for 0.4 mile, then turn left and park in the UNH parking lot.

RIDE DIRECTIONS

0.0 Left out of the parking lot on Hackett Hill Road.

2.5 Left on South Bow Road.

6.4 At stop sign/T, turn left on Woodhill Road (unmarked).

7.1 Right on Morse Road.

7.8 At stop sign, turn left on Montelona Road.

11.2 Right on Tirrell Hill Road.

12.1 At 4-way stop sign, right on Black Brook Road (unmarked).
At 12.9 miles on right, notice the marsh. Keep an eye out for great blue herons.

15.7 At Y, stay left (straight)—still on Black Brook Road.

17.0 At stop sign T, go left on Black Brook Road (unmarked, there's a large boulder at this turn).

17.8 At stop sign, turn right on Route 13N (unmarked). This road has moderate volume, fast traffic and a long downhill (after the long uphill).
At about 19.5 miles you enter Dunbarton center.
At 20.4-mile point on left, the granite

Stonehenge-like structure is the town pound built in 1791 to corral stray animals.

22.3   **Left on Winslow Road.**
There's a country store at this turn. For the next four or five miles follow signs for Clough State Park.

23.0   **Left at fork on Stark Lane.**

23.8   **At stop sign/T, turn left on Mansion Street.**

25.1   **Right, follow Everett Dam/Clough State Park signs. This road is hidden by trees, so watch for it closely.**
At about 26.4 miles is the entrance to Clough State Park—a good place to stop and swim.

At about 26.7 miles is the Everett Dam gate. Take a break here for a nice view.

28.6   **At stop sign/T, left on River Road (unmarked).**

31.3   **Left at stop sign on River Road (becomes Parker Station Rd.).**

32.5   **Right on 114N.**

32.7   **Left on Parker Road.**

33.6   **Left at fork, over bridge, then left at T on Route 13 (unmarked).**
At 34.0 miles is an optional ice cream stop on the left—Putnam's Waterview Restaurant and Pizza.

35.9   **At stop sign in Goffstown, go left on Route 114.**

36.2   **Right on Elm Street. Caution: fast traffic with no shoulder.**
At this corner is a Civil War statue. If you like popcorn, the world-famous Goffstown Popcorn Stand is across the street by the grocery store.

39.3   **Bear left at fork on Goffstown Back Road.**
Grasmere Convenience Store here.

42.2   **Sharp hairpin left on Straw Road.**

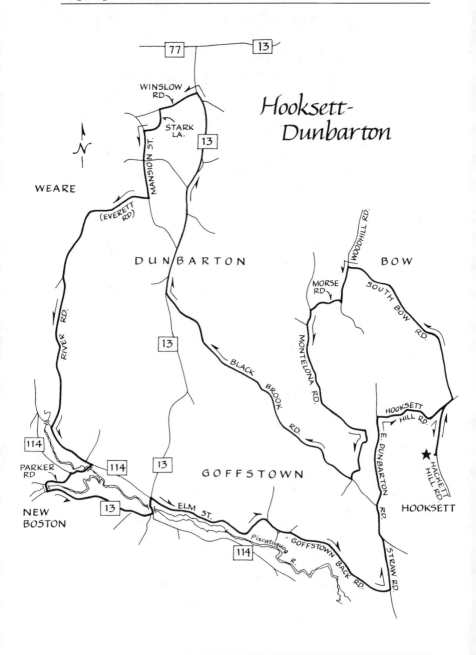

Hooksett-
Dunbarton

43.3	Left at stop sign on Dunbarton Road.
43.9	At Y, stay right on East Dunbarton Road.
44.9	At Y, stay straight on East Dunbarton Road (unmarked).
45.9	Right on Hooksett Hill Road.
47.4	At stop sign, go right on Hackett Hill Road.
49.6	Right into UNH parking lot.

16 GOFFSTOWN–MILFORD

42.3 miles
Rolling, with a number of moderate
hills, several steep climbs, and a
one-mile stretch of well-packed gravel

B eguiling cities that seem more like small towns in warmth and hospitality. The hub of business, finance and government. The lifeblood of culture and the arts. This is Merrimack Valley. More than half the population of New Hampshire lives in the Merrimack Valley region, yet only minutes from any large city will bring you to tranquil forests, clear streams, and excellent cycling roads.

This bicycling tour is particularly beautiful during fall foliage season in early October when leaves display their tawny autumn shades. It's delightful too, on a breezy summer day when you chance upon the pink-and-white color burst of mountain laurel.

The tour begins in the bedroom community of Goffstown—within blocks of Manchester, the American counterpart of its British namesake and the state's largest city.

The tour leaves from St. Anselm's College Dana Center parking lot. St. Anselm's is a well-respected liberal arts college founded in 1889. If time allows, take a few minutes and cross the campus to the Chapel Art Center, which hosts 12 exhibitions each year (open during academic year, Monday through Friday, 10–4). Works by local and regional artists and traveling exhibitions are featured.

If you want to immerse yourself in more art, consider a side trip to downtown Manchester to the Currier Gallery. The Currier is considered one of the finest small museums in America. Its rich collections span the 13th through 20th centuries, featuring works of world-renowned artists.

This ride soon finds you pedaling along the Piscataquog River to New Boston, where the town square burned down in 1880. When it was rebuilt, the buildings were predictably Victorian. It's a quintessential New England town square with Dodge's Store, a classic white church, and even the Molly Stark Cannon. The historic cannon is housed in a small building on the common.

If your timing is right, you may cycle through this area when New Boston hosts the Hillsborough County Agricultural Fair in early September or the New Hampshire Sheep and Wool Festival on Mother's Day weekend.

Traveling south to Mont Vernon, a hilltop town overlooking the Souhegan Valley, you'll experience the cycling highlight of the trip as you glide down a long, sinuous hill and take in the panoramic view. While in Mont Vernon, several buildings are worth noting. Among them is the colonial town hall, built in 1781. Across the street from the town hall is the Congregational Church with its fieldstone construction, stained glass windows, and a picture-perfect pastoral setting at the crest of a hill.

From Mont Vernon the route continues south through a corner of Milford, where you might catch a glimpse of the Hot Air Balloon Show at the end of June. Milford, long known as the Granite Town of the Granite State because of its voluminous quarrying of granite, is also the proud owner of one of the oldest Paul Revere bells. It tolls faithfully in the belfry of the Town House clock tower every hour.

Traveling on to Amherst, a gracious, historic New England town, you may want to stop by the library for a walking-tour pamphlet. The town common is surrounded by fine examples of Palladian architecture, Greek revival doorways, colonial and Victorian architecture, and of course, Federal-style homes.

As you leave Amherst center, you pass by an architectural gem from the Federalist period with double dentil molding under the eaves and an extra wide "coffin door." In 1834 Franklin Pierce, 14th President of the United States, was married here to Jane Means Appleton. Also at the east end of the Big Common is the Second County Courthouse where in 1805 Daniel Webster made his maiden plea (i.e., plead his first case as an attorney before a judge).

Shortly after leaving Amherst village you pass Horace Greeley's birth place. Greeley, born here in 1811, made famous the phrase "Go west, young man, go west," was also known as the Granite State's most famous journalist, congressman, and presidential candidate.

Even though Merrimack Valley is one of the most populated areas in the state, you'll never know it by the roads you'll be cycling today.

RIDE INFORMATION

Highlights: Panoramic view of Souhegan Valley, historic Amherst with Franklin Pierce house, scenic ride along Piscatoquog River, a swimming hole, Horace Greeley's birth home.

Start: St. Anselm's College parking lot in Goffstown. To get there take Route 101W. In Bedford at the intersection of Route 101 and Route 114, continue straight on Route 114N toward Goffstown for two stop lights. Right on St. Anselm Drive. In a mile, take the first right after College Road. Sign here says Dana Center. Park in parking lot on left.

RIDE DIRECTIONS

0.0   From parking lot, turn left on St. Anselm Drive.

1.1   At stop light at Route 114, cross the road to Shirley Hill Road.

2.8   **Right on Wallace Road (unmarked).**
After a half-mile uphill climb, you'll begin a two-mile gradual descent.

5.6   At stop sign, left on South Mast Street/Route 114. This is a busy, high-traffic road with minimal shoulder.

A welcome sign, indeed ...

6.2   Left on Route 13S.

This stretch of road follows the Piscataquog River. As you cycle past corn fields, you'll see historic markers (one at 8.6 miles) in honor of Charles Davis, a Vietnam veteran for whom the road is named—Davis Scenic Drive. Around 9.3 miles is a large rock slab for picnicking, sunning, or swimming.

12.9   Right at stop sign on the New Boston Town Common, past Dodge's Store for 0.1 mile and then over the bridge to stop sign.

Dodge's Store is an old country store with a spacious front porch, slate roof and worn, wooden floors. Cool off here with Italian ice, Ben and Jerry's ice cream, or juice.

Adjacent to the store is the common. Near the town hall is a small, white building with green trim. The Molly Stark Cannon is housed here. A Revolutionary victory relic of the 1776 Battle of Bennington, the cannon, which has unique decorations of Indians, bows and arrows, and a shield and crown, has a mate in the Museum of Artillery at Woolwich in London, England.

13.0   Left at stop sign—still on Route 13S (Mont Vernon Road). Caution: This road has fast traffic, storm grates and no shoulder.

Shortly after this turn you'll see The Molly Stark Tavern on your left. It is well known for its tasty food.

As you enter Mont Vernon, there are a number of antique stores to satisfy the antique enthusiast.

Mont Vernon has its share of beautiful Victorian homes with wrap-around porches, turrets, and ornate decorations, as well as Federal-style colonials with their symmetrical facades and double chimneys. Note the colonial town hall built in 1781 and the Congregational Church made of fieldstone.

As you leave Mont Vernon, you begin a steep mile-long, downhill. If that isn't enough of a treat, you receive the added benefit of a panoramic view of the Souhegan Valley. Enjoy the scenery!

23.4   At stop sign, go left—continuing on Route 13S. You're now in Milford.

23.9   At stop sign, go straight across for 0.1 mile.

24.0   At stop sign, continue straight on Grove Street (Amherst Rd./Route 122).

26.2   Left on Main Street to village of Amherst.
In Amherst there's a convenience store for an ice cream stop. Keep the "Big Common" to your left.

You may wish to stop at the Amherst Library (before Village Green Market) on right and pick up a brochure for a self-guided tour of historic Amherst. (These are private homes and not open to the public.)

At the end of the common on the right is the house with double dentil molding where Franklin Pierce married Jane Means Appleton.

26.5   At fork, stay left. You'll immediately pass the town hall—a brick building on right. Pass between the brown house and a white two-story columned house on the left. (Sign here says Manchester St. A very short way later, road becomes Mack Hill Road. Stay straight on Mack Hill.)

28.7   Right on Austin Road.
This winding road becomes gravel after half a mile. But the mile of gravel is packed and easily traveled.

30.4   **At stop sign/T , turn left on Horace Greeley Road (unmarked).**
Cider Mill Country Store is in front of you at this T-intersection.

31.6   **Stay right at Y, still on Horace Greeley Road.**
At about 32.9 miles you begin a short uphill climb. On the left is an old barn with rough-hewn vertical siding, lots of stone walls, and a nondescript small house near the road. A plaque on a rock in front of the house commemorates Horace Greeley's birthplace. It's now a private home.

33.2   **The road you're on intersects with Joppa Hill Road. Cross Joppa Hill Road and continue straight on North Amherst Road.**

36.2   **Left on Wallace Road.**
Immediately upon turning on Wallace Road, you begin to go uphill and uphill and uphill. Eventually you're rewarded for your effort with scenic views of attractive farms, nice homes, and stone walls. Hang on—there's also a long descent!

38.0   **At stop sign/blinker continue straight—still on Wallace Road.**
This stretch of road is spectacular during the summer when the mountain laurel is in full bloom.

39.5   **At stop sign, turn right on Shirley Hill Road (unmarked).**

41.2   **At stop light on Route 114, cross the road to St. Anselm Drive.**

42.3   **Right, back on St. Anselm campus.**

17 BEDFORD

21.4 miles
Challenging, a few tough hills,
some moderate climbs

Quaint and uncluttered with a historic hilltop center highlighted by a white-steepled, gold-domed church, gracious older homes and the architecturally-handsome Greek Revival Town Hall, Bedford is an unhurried community that exudes a vivid sense of the past.

Once a rural community that provided produce for neighboring city Manchester, Bedford is now mostly home to professionals and their families.

The ride starts at Bedford Center's common. Here the Bedford Library, established in 1789, resides. It's "down the road a piece" from the hilltop-home of the Presbyterian Church. Dedicated in 1832, the 400-seat church has strong roots in Calvinism.

The clock that graces the steeple was purchased from the E. Howard Clock Company of Boston. It's wound once a week by a lever which raises a wooden box of crushed stones. Carefully selected, the stones provide the proper weight so the large timepiece will keep precise time for seven days. The clock is still wound by hand today. In 1894, Alexander Wadsworth Longfellow of Boston, nephew of the famous poet, was the architect responsible for the design of the front porch with its classic columns, as well as other redecoration appointments.

As you pedal west, the ride passes an exotic fowl sanctuary, gracious homes from Federal and Georgian eras, and a number of well-preserved stone walls. Soon you come upon the Evans mansion. On a hillside with a reflecting pond below, the mansion is a private home purported to be worth $4.5 million.

Passing near Bedford Village Shoppes, a compact nest of boutiques and restaurants, you'll soon be surrounded by open farmland. Cows graze on nearby hillsides. They glance your way as you cycle past. Disinterested, they soon return to munching clumps of grass.

Educationally oriented, the Marconi Museum, which you pass on this ride, contains thousands of radio communications periodicals, equipment, and historical gadgets. An audio-visual presentation on Marconi, the Father of Radio, explains the development of radio from "sparks to space."

Turning on Joppa Hill Road, you'll work (yes, you do work, folks!) your way through an apple orchard and then coast down two steep inclines. (Yes, yes!)

Although Bedford is surrounded by busy thoroughfares, this tour avoids them and keeps you in the gently rolling countryside.

RIDE INFORMATION

Highlights: Historic colonial buildings, exotic fowl sanctuary, Marconi Museum, innumerable stone walls, $4.5 million Evans mansion, and picture-perfect New England scenery.

Start: Bedford Center Library in Bedford Center. From the intersection of Routes 114/101, head west on Route 101 for 1.2 miles to stop light. Go right at stop light up the hill for 0.2 mile to the library on the left.

RIDE DIRECTIONS

0.0   **Right out of library parking lot to stop light. Cross**

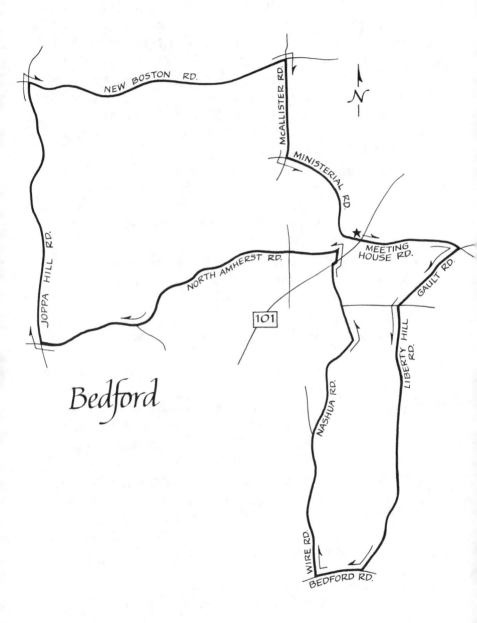

Bedford

intersection at light, to Meeting House Road.

1.1   Right on Gault Road.

2.0   Left on Liberty Hill Road (to become Pearson Road). Just beyond the southern brick colonial at about 3.5 miles, on the right, an exotic bird sanctuary encompasses the corner. Here preening peacocks, common pheasants, wood ducks, guinea fowl, and barnyard hens strut around their landscaped space.

5.5   At stop sign, go right on Bedford Road (unmarked).

6.1   At stop sign, turn right on Wire Road (to become Nashua Road).

8.1   Turn right—still on Nashua Road.
      Great stone walls along here!

      When you near the 8.4-mile mark, the Evans mansion will loom on the distant knoll on the right. Shortly after the mansion, on the left a homey, brick colonial built in 1888 symbolizes a less-hurried lifestyle of days past.

10.1 Stop sign. Here at Route 101 intersection, cross the road diagonally to right to Bell Hill Road. Left on Bell Hill Road.

      If you take a left here on 101 instead of crossing to Bell Hill Road, you can travel a short way to Bedford Village Shoppes, an enticing network of boutiques, gourmet shops, and yummy eateries.

      On your left after you cross Route 101 is Bell Hill Antiques. It has rooms full of little treasures!

10.2 Left on North Amherst Road.

10.3 Stop sign. Go left, still on Amherst Road. (The Flower Cart is in front of you. After the turn, the Marconi Museum is a short distance up this road on the left.)

      This road has several long, moderate climbs. They'll prepare you for Joppa Hill Road.

13.7 **Right on Joppa Hill Road by Joppa Hill Farm.**
This working farm and apple orchard has several long, gradual climbs interspersed with two steep descents. This is the most challenging three miles of the trip.

The stone walls along this stretch of road are beautifully aged.

At about the 15.2-mile mark as you crest a long hill, your efforts will be rewarded with a view of Mount Uncanoonuc ahead.

If you chance to take this ride at the right time during the summer, you'll be delighted to find mountain laurel in full bloom around 16.2 miles.

16.5 **At stop sign, turn right on New Boston Road.**
This road has light, but fast-moving traffic. There's a narrow shoulder that ends periodically.

19.2 **Right on McAllister Road.**

20.2 **At stop sign, turn left on Ministerial Road.**

21.3 **At Y intersection, bear left on Church Road. Then there's another Y intersection. Stay to right.**

21.4 **Library is on the right.**

18 MERRIMACK

16 miles
Gently rolling

L ocated along the river that is its namesake, Merrimack is home to a number of industrial powerhouses. It boasts some of the most noteworthy corporations in New Hampshire—PC Connection, Fidelity Investments, Unitrode Corporation, Chemfab Corporation, and Anheuser-Busch.

Although the area where the tour begins has a lot of traffic, you're quickly on roads with few cars. They meander past attractive new homes, old New England barns, grazing horses, and quiet marsh land. The roads, for the most part, are flat.

You may want to allow time after the ride to tour the Anheuser-Busch brewery, sample some of the brewmasters wares, stop by the gift and sportswear shop, and check out the white-stockinged Clydesdale horses. The world's largest brewery, Anheuser-Busch produces three million barrels of beer a year (31 gallons per barrel). Complimentary tours are available daily 10–4, May through October. Open Thursday through Monday 10–4, November through April.

RIDE INFORMATION

Highlights: Anheuser-Busch Brewery, attractive residential areas with very little traffic.

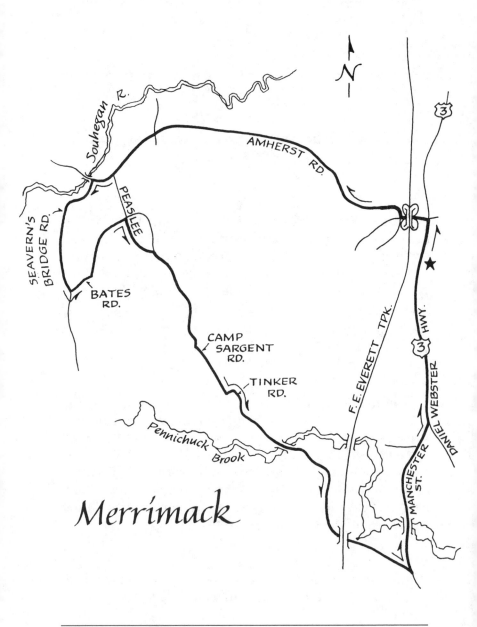

Start: Anheuser-Busch parking lot. Take exit 11 from the Everett Turnpike. The brewery is on Route 3 between Nashua and Manchester—on left, about a mile from the exit.

RIDE DIRECTIONS

0.0 **Left out of parking lot by stop sign and up driveway to Route 3.**

0.2 **Right on Route 3N.**
This is a very busy road, but it has wide breakdown lanes.

All along this strip are places to eat, everything from McDonald's to the popular Hannah Jack Restaurant (homestead of Matthew Thornton, signer of the Declaration of Independence).

1.1 **Left at traffic light, toward Everett turnpike, and then *under* the turnpike.**

1.4 **Right at light on Amherst Road (unmarked—Burker King in front of you here.)**
If you're starving or need liquid refreshment now or after the trip, there's a Burger King and D'Angelo's Sub Shop here.

5.3 **Left on Seavern's Bridge Road.**
This turn is just before a bridge which spans the Souhegan River.

6.6 **Left on Bates Road (unmarked). There's a large boulder on left at this turn.**

7.7 **At stop sign, turn right on Peaslee Road. (Becomes Naticook Road.)**

9.4 **At stop sign, go left on Camp Sargent Road.**

9.5 **At Y, stay right on Tinker Road.**

9.8 **At stop light, stay straight.**

10.7 **At Y, stay left.**
At 10.9 miles on right is a pleasant area for a stop

beside tall pines and a calm pond.

13.0   At stop sign, turn left on Manchester Street.

14.5   At stop sign, turn left on Daniel Webster Highway (Route 3N).

15.8   Right into upper entrance of Anheuser-Busch.

16.0   Turn right into parking lot, where you began your tour.

19 HOLLIS

8.7 miles or 17.4 miles
Rolling, hilly terrain with one long,
gradual hill

E ven in burgeoning southern New Hampshire you can still find a sense of peace and tranquility. It's evident in the Massachusetts border town of Hollis with its rolling landscape, forested areas, open vistas, brooks, ponds, and country fragrances. Whether it's in the historic town common of Hollis or the serenity of Maple Hill Farm at Beaver Brook Association, this bike tour will help balance your sense of priorities.

Visiting the center of Hollis is like discovering yesterday. It's an attractive New England village where the past has been preserved by those who appreciate their heritage and are determined to protect it.

The common has wonderful colonial buildings worth noting. The Hollis Social Library, where the tour begins, is an impressive structure built in 1779. To its right is the Congregational Church and burial grounds, and across the common is the Town Hall with its distinctive clock tower.

As the ride heads out of town, you'll encounter corn fields in perfect soldier order, apple orchards dressed in pink blossoms or burdened with this year's apple growth, and quiet, deserted roads that entice you to pedal on.

Soon you'll find your way to the haven known as Maple

Hill Farm. A part of Beaver Brook Association, a 1,600-acre greenbelt with 26 miles of nature trails for hiking, Maple Hill Farm invites people to learn more about their natural environment and to realize the interdependence of people and nature. Annuals and perennial plantings grace the open spaces and encourage you to sit a spell and have a picnic lunch on the grounds.

Near the end of the tour is Silver Lake State Park—another super place for a picnic. A public beach and a playground here invite you to make a day of it with your family. Ride the tour in the morning, have a picnic lunch at Maple Hill Farm or at the state park, and then cool off in the lake for the afternoon.

RIDE INFORMATION

Highlights: Historical Monument Square area of Hollis, Maple Hill Farm (part of Beaver Brook Association—a conservation area with nature trails and exhibit building), and Silver Lake State Park with swimming and picnicking areas.

Start: Hollis village common. Take Route 130W off the Everett Turnpike (exit 6) for 5.3 miles. Route 130W bears right, but continue straight for 0.4 mile to the village common. Park along the common or in front of the library.

RIDE DIRECTIONS

0.0   **Start in front of the library. Go to the right of the common to a stop sign across the street from the town hall with the clock tower. Then go right on Depot Road (unmarked).**

2.8   **Right on Twiss Lane.**

3.8   **At stop sign, go left on Dow Road.**

3.9   **Right on Blood Road.**

4.8   At stop sign, turn right on Pepperell Road (Route 122), take immediate left on Worcester Road.

6.0   Right on Ridge Road.

At about 6.1 miles there's packed gravel for a mile. This road has a classic stone wall flanked by full, spreading oak trees.

At about 6.9 miles Maple Hill Farm (Beaver Brook Association) is on the left. It's a gray farmhouse with white trim, number 117. Take a walk on the grounds and smell the flowers.

8.1   At stop sign, left on Main Street/Pepperell Road (Route 122S).

On the left at this turn, don't miss the weathered burial ground on the hill. Main Street in Hollis has some stately two- and four-chimneyed Federal-style colonial homes with aged bricks and tall white fences.

***

Note: If you want to make this a short ride, turn right by the Always Ready Engine House at about 8.7 miles, and you'll be back at the common.

***

9.0   At traffic light, go left on Route 130W for 0.5 mile to Rocky Pond Road.

9.5   Turn right on Rocky Pond Road. Note: You're in a rapid descent just before the right turn onto Rocky Pond Road. Slow down so you don't miss the turn.

At about 11.2 miles on left is Rocky Pond. It's a pretty area for a break, a swim, or a picnic. In early to mid-May keep an eye out for nesting great blue herons.

11.4   At T-intersection, turn right on Hayden Road. Note: Slow down on the long descent near the 13.8-mile mark, as a stop sign appears soon.

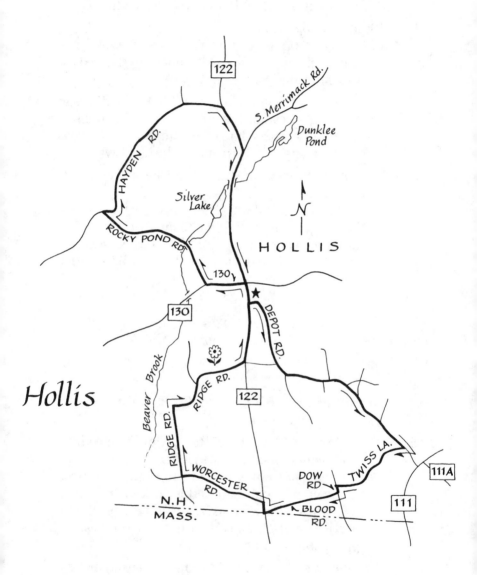

Hollis

14.0   **At stop sign, go right on Route 122S (unmarked).** This fast-paced traffic road has no shoulder. With any luck, you'll travel through Woodmont Apple Orchard during peak apple blossom season. Silver Lake State Park is at 15.8 miles—in case it's a sweltering day and you're ready for a dip.

17.1   **At stop light, continue straight—still on Route 122S.**

17.3   **Left by Always Ready Engine House (Ash Street—but unmarked) for 0.1 mile to library.**

The Always Ready Engine House is the oldest public building in Hollis, built in 1859. It now houses the Hollis Always Ready Pump, circa 1858, and the town hearse, circa 1868.

Just up the street from the engine house is the a country store. The owners will gladly help you find your way to such refreshments as apple-cherryberry juice, which bears no historical significance whatsoever.

17.4   **Library on left.**

20 GILMANTON-LOUDON

23.9 or 32.0 miles,
3 miles of hard-packed gravel
Hilly, numerous steep uphills, challenging

Gilmanton, New Hampshire, is a rural community located above Concord. A quiet New England village, it boasts some fine colonial buildings, and a historic inn.

Leaving from the town center, you travel to Gilmanton Ironworks, then the ride skirts into a corner of Loudon. This cycling tour is through some of the most scenic countryside you'll ever want to see. The tranquility and peacefulness is addicting. As you zip along, you soon regret the thought of soon having to go back to "real life." Just remember this is part of what makes it all worthwhile!

Truly not for the less-seasoned rider, this tour gives your leg muscles a serious workout. Numerous hills are sprinkled throughout the ride. But the payoff is breathtaking views, a great workout, and a day of riding with virtually no traffic.

Don't be entirely put off because this ride seems too difficult. You can always walk your bike! It's allowed. Remember, you're still getting exercise. You're still indulging in the beauty unique to New Hampshire. And remember, this is what recharges our batteries to go back and fight the battle. So, just do it!

RIDE INFORMATION

Highlights: A terrific tour. Virtually no traffic. Peaceful backroads, old burying grounds, stone walls, panoramic vistas, grazing horses and cows, melodic streams, sparkling lakes, possible moose sitings. A bit hilly, but all worth it for the peaceful scenery.

Start: Gilmanton Town Hall at intersection of Rte. 107 and 140.

RIDE DIRECTIONS

0.0 **Park behind Gilmanton Town Hall. Left out of the driveway to the stop light, and go left on 140E. Prepare to climb for half a mile.**

Across from the town hall is the historic three-story Temperance B&B, a handsome 1793 homestead, it has served as an inn for over 200 years. It features original 18th century stenciling.

A country store at this intersection is jam-packed with all kinds of yummies.

4.0 **Left on Middle Route.**

At 6.3 miles on the right is a mini water fall. Stop for a short break. At 6.5 miles a pond on the right often has moose sitings. Also this road has a time-worn burying ground with lichen-covered stones.

7.0 **Right at Y on Sargent Rd. (unmarked). This road becomes Guinea Ridge Road and then Crystal Lake Road—all unmarked. You will encounter three miles of hard-packed gravel—easily maneuvered on bike.**

At 8.1 miles by the yellow farm house, look to your right. A gorgeous panoramic view. Perfect for fall viewing!

At 10.0 miles, another old burying ground.

11.3 **Stay straight (not the road that goes to your left).**

A water stop is appropriate at 11.8 miles with Crystal Lake flanking both sides of the road.

14.5 **At stop sign/T-intersection, turn left on Rte. 140 (unmarked.).**

14.9 **Right on Stage Road.**
Iron Works Market is at this intersection. Ice cream stop!

16.2 **At Y, bear left.**
This road goes up and up and up. Don't complain—you're getting exercise! Burning calories, reducing cellulite, you know. Just buck up and do it!

19.4 **At stop sign/T-intersection, left on Rte. 107S (unmarked).**

***

If you would like to shorten this ride, go right here on Rte. 107N and it will take you back to Gilmanton Center.

***

20.1 **Right on Rte. 129W.**

23.2 **Right on Loudon Ridge Road.**
Swear now and be done in advance—there are some nasty, steep uphills on this road. But also calming streams, grazing cattle and horses, and waving cornfields. Life's a balance!

After a tough climb, at 24.3 miles, gaze to your left—and see for miles. Misty mountain peaks loom in the distance. Tree tops turn brilliant colors (in the fall). And you can be glad you live in New Hampshire (or are visiting!).

Pick up a few ears of sweet corn or other fresh veggies at the Windswept Maples Farm at 27.3 miles.

28.5 **At stop sign/T, turn right on Rte. 106 (unmarked).**

29.3 Right on Allen's Mills Road. This begins a very looooong uphill.

31.3 At stop sign/T, right on Rte. 140 (unmarked).

31.9 Left on Rte. 107N.

32.0 Right into town hall driveway.

21 STRAFFORD– BOW LAKE

9.5 miles
Mostly rolling with two, long uphills,
lots of downhills

This is it, folks! The perfect family ride. It's short—only 9.5 miles. It's manageable terrain—well, two long up-hills—but jump off your bikes and walk. It's an excellent opportunity for quality time. And there's no traffic! You'll have to try this ride around Bow Lake to believe it.

If all that's not ideal *enough*, add stone walls, large maples, birches, tree-canopied roads, and old burial grounds with granite slab walls. And if you choose to ride in early June, you'll see gazillions of wild purple iris.

Strafford, a rural, off-the-beaten-path village, was primarily an agricultural community, according to early area histories. Farming and lumbering were the chief occupations. Rye and corn were grown for feed, pigs were raised for meat, cows for milk, butter, and meat. Flax was grown for linen. Sheep supplied wool and meat, and geese were raised for food, but especially for down, to stuff beds and pillows. Apple orchards were also a source of food and income. Other industries included sawmills, a shoe manu-facturer, and a shoebox factory. But not anymore. Strafford is a bedroom community for Concord, but mostly it's sequestered away like a hidden jewel—exactly what the locals want it to be. Undiscovered.

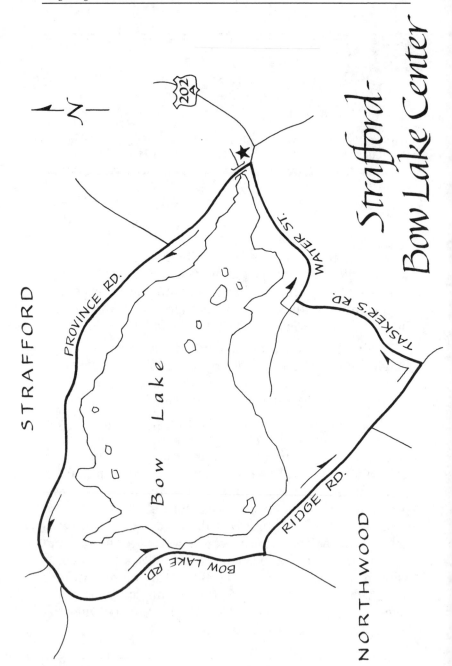

Strafford-
Bow Lake Center

RIDE INFORMATION

Highlights: A beautiful ride that circles around the lake—with a place for a picnic and swimming at the end of the ride. Pretty water fall. Near Northwood for antiquing. Six old burial grounds on tour. See if you can find all six.

Start: Bow Lake Center Grange Parking lot. To get there, take Route 202 east in Northwood for 0.3 mile, then left on Route 202A east for 3.4 miles to stop sign. At stop sign, left for 0.1 mile—white Grange building straight ahead—across from Thorne's Market.

RIDE DIRECTIONS

0.0 Left out of the Bow Lake Center Grange parking lot on Province Road (unmarked).

Thorne's Market is across the street (for snacks).

To the right of the Grange building is a water fall.

At the 0.4-mile point on right is Berrybogg Farm—stop and pick some fresh berries for blueberry crisp tonight!

3.2 Stay left (a sign here says Northwood Road).

5.9 At T, turn left on Sideburn Hill Rd. (This sign is mislabeled. The road's correct name is Sherburne Hill Road. It becomes Bow Lake Rd.).

7.0 At T, follow the arrow to right, Ridge Road.

7.5 Left on Tasker Road.

8.4 At stop sign T, turn right. (This is Water Street, but it is unmarked. A sign on left side of the pole says Brown's Pasture Road—for the road on the left.)

9.5 Circle around the Bow Lake Center Grange building on the left and back into the parking lot.

22 NORTHWOOD– NOTTINGHAM

23.2 miles
Moderately difficult. One long, tough hill,
a few quick hills and numerous long, gradual climbs

T his tour will be a taste of heaven to those who love antiquing. Northwood is a mecca for antiques, collectibles, and country crafts. The antique shops abound along Route 4 between Epsom and Northwood—and so does the traffic. Fortunately, your bike tour encompasses less than two miles of this busy thoroughfare—the majority of the ride finds you cycling along tree-canopied roads, past working farms, and through pastoral villages.

Soon after your ride begins, you enter Deerfield Parade, where large houses and the imposing Prescott Tavern (1800) abut the parade grounds (used by militia during the Revolutionary and Civil Wars), a reminder that a prosperous commercial and postal center existed here during the early 19th century.

Nottingham Road, which flanks the back side of Pawtuckaway State Park, takes you past several colonial homes built in the mid-1700s. In early to mid-June you may happen upon snapping turtles nesting in sandy areas adjacent to bridges. (The author saw two immense females nesting within a few hundred yards of each other.) If you encounter them, observe them but do not disturb them. They may abandon their nest. Bear in mind also that they can effortlessly snap off your finger.

Traveling on past a large cattle farm, you cycle into Nottingham Square. And shortly after that, you're back in Northwood.

RIDE INFORMATION

Highlights: "Antique Alley" in Northwood, two historic markers, historic Deerfield Parade and several 1700s colonial homes, lots of quiet country roads, Nottingham Schoolhouse Museum, and Nottingham Historical Society.

Start: Northwood office of the Bank of New Hampshire. If you're on Route 4 heading east from Concord, it's on the right a half mile before Route 43. Park behind the bank on the side with the split rail fence. This is a commuter parking lot.

RIDE DIRECTIONS

0.0 **Right out of the bank parking lot on Route 4E.**
There is a wide shoulder on this busy road.

0.5 **Right on Route 43S by library.**
Route 43S has moderate, but fast moving traffic—and no shoulder. There are several long, gradual climbs on this road.

6.4 **Left on Route 107/43S.**
At this intersection there's a convenience store where you can find homemade bear claws, fig bars, Danish, and other goodies.

At 7.1 miles on the right, note the Major John Simpson historical marker. He fired the first— and unauthorized—shot at Bunker Hill. Reprimanded for his initiative at the time, his birthplace is now memorialized.

7.3 **Left on Nottingham Road toward Deerfield Parade.**
As you turn, on the right is a historic marker

explaining the colonial settling of Deerfield Parade, which was on the early postal route between Concord and Portsmouth. The militia of the Revolutionary and Civil Wars trained and "paraded" on the village common.

෴෴෴

Northwood-Nottingham

7.4   **Bear right at Y intersection.**

Soon you begin a long, moderate but steady uphill climb. This is a pretty, *pretty* road. You'll see mountain views off to your right, nice homes, well-kept farms with goats munching on grass, a granite-slab fence around an old cemetery, and stately, mature maples.

8.1   **Bear right at Y intersection still on Nottingham Road (unmarked). Sign at village common in front of you reads "Deerfield Parade."**

Here on your right are two circa 1800 buildings—the Prescott Tavern and the General Store. This is a wonderfully deserted, tree-canopied backroad with a few climbs and an arduous uphill. On the backside of Pawtuckaway State Park, it becomes Deerfield Road in Nottingham. For a sweeping, panoramic view, look to the left at 11.6 miles (near a gray mobile home).

Pay attention to several well-preserved colonial homes built in the 1700s along this road. And if you appreciate time-seasoned cemeteries with wrought iron gates, stone walls, and tombstones like those in textbooks on colonial New England, you'll be pleased to find three of these old burial grounds along this road.

14.9   **At stop sign at Nottingham Square, turn left on Route 156N.**

If you have time, take in the Schoolhouse Museum, Nottingham Historical Society, and the Old Village Common.

16.0   **At the stop sign, turn left on Route 152W.**

Fast, low-volume traffic. No shoulder. At about 20.9 miles, Olde Crossroads Store is a good stop-off place for refreshments.

At 21.4 miles on the right is Sherwood Park—in

Nottingham—beware of stray arrows!

21.9 **At stop sign, turn left on Route 4W.**
You're back at extremely busy Route 4. It is four lanes at this point, so cyclists do fine when they keep to the right.

23.2 **Back where you began at the Bank of New Hampshire on the left.**

23 AUBURN–DEERFIELD

48.6 miles
Difficult, very hilly, one steep hill

J ust east of Manchester, the urban area thins out quickly into quiet suburban neighborhoods and rolling hills dotted with stately colonial homes. This tour skirts rural farmland and picture postcard scenes of spreading maple trees, towering silos, and verdant corn fields.

Lake Massabesic in Auburn marks the start of the tour. In its heyday, Auburn was to New Hampshire what Camden is to Maine. The chic Boston summer crowd flocked to Auburn's summer hotels. They vied for a chance to cruise Lake Massabesic on the "Winnie L," a double decker steamship that carried 100 passengers and offered a generous dance floor. Badminton, croquet, and kite-flying were also favorite pastimes of the Boston elite. These sophisticated urbanites acquired a fondness for the beauty and simplicity of the New Hampshire country life that endures today.

The ride leaves Auburn and meanders through Candia. Although Candia is relatively close to the city—only 12 miles east of Manchester—its antique colonial homes and rambling stone walls provide the ambiance of an ideal rural community. Candia offers gentle woods, small farms, and its own slice of history.

You cycle past Candia Woods Golf Course and through an

affluent neighborhood where well-maintained, old New England farmhouses are set off by expansive shade trees and moss-covered stone walls. The village center is exceptionally appealing with a historic, white-clapboarded, black-shuttered Congregational church. Nearby a war monument stands as a reminder of those who've died in service to our country.

Approaching Deerfield, you travel past open farmland and sweeping expanses of green space and soon you cycle past the Deerfield Fairgrounds. The fair is New England's oldest county fair. Held late September, it offers agricultural exhibits, a fairway, competitions, and entertainment. Based on whether you love fried dough and farm animals or hate traffic congestion and crowds, you can decide if you want to choose this ride in late September. Happy trails!

RIDE INFORMATION

Highlights: Scenic lake with picnic area, pond and stream views, historic buildings, Deerfield Fair.

Start: Lake Massabesic picnic area in Auburn. Take exit 1 (Auburn/Hooksett) on Route 101 just east of Manchester. Turn south toward the traffic circle. Travel half-way around circle—taking Bypass 28 South. Turn left and park in picnic area or designated area on road.

RIDE DIRECTIONS

0.0 **Turn right out of the Lake Massabesic picnic area toward the traffic circle. Go a quarter of the way around the circle, then right on Route 121E.**

On the left at 1.2 miles resides a long, white house with the date 1835 over the door. It's the Smith House—the only former summer hotel in Auburn still owned and lived in by descendents of the original family.

2.9 **At the intersection, continue straight on Raymond**

Road. A large Victorian house will be on your right.

3.2   **Bear right on Eaton Road.** This road has a half-mile uphill climb, followed by a downhill glide.

4.9   **At stop sign, turn left on Chester Turnpike.**

7.1   **At four-way intersection, turn right on Old Candia Road.**

8.2   **Left on South Road (unmarked—it's just after you go over a bridge).**

8.4   **At stop sign, turn left—still on South Road—past Candia Woods Golf Course.**
Along this road are stately colonial homes, elegantly landscaped with immense maples, dignified birches, and long-needled pines. And, of course, stone walls.

10.1 **At the stop sign, cross Route 27 to Healey Road.**
The Candia Congregational Church, organized in 1771, is located at this corner. Across the street is a war monument.

10.8 **At stop sign, bear left on North Road.**

12.4 **At four-way stop sign intersection, turn right on New Boston Road (unmarked).**

14.7 **At stop sign, turn left on Route 43N (unmarked). This road has fast traffic, no shoulder.**
You'll soon begin a half-mile uphill climb. Papa's Country Store is on left during the climb—in case you need a refreshment stop.

16.1 **At T junction, turn right, still on Route 43N.**
At about the 17.7-mile mark, Deerfield Fairground is on your right.

18.5 **At stop sign, turn right on Route 107S, a gently rolling road with little traffic.**

22.3 **At stop sign, go left on Route 27E, a road with moderately heavy, fast traffic.**

24.0 **Take a sharp right at Langford Road.**

24.8   Left on Onway Lake Road.

26.1   At T/ stop sign by rock quarry, turn left on Scribner Road (unmarked) to a stop sign, then left on Gile Road.

C3C3C3

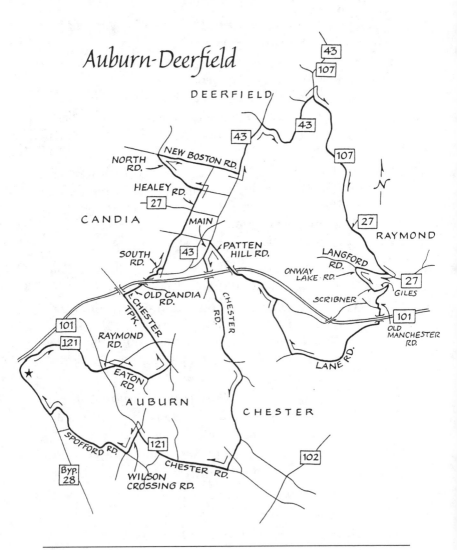

26.6   **Right at stop sign on Old Manchester Road (unmarked).**

27.1   **At T stop sign, turn right on Lane Road.**

29.0   **At Y, stay straight—still on Lane Road.**

32.0   **At four-way stop sign, turn left on Patten Hill Road.**
Soon there's a very steep, long hill.

34.5   **At stop sign/T-intersection, turn left on Main Street (unmarked).**

34.9   **Left on Chester Road.**

41.1   **At stop sign/T-intersection, turn right on Route 121 (unmarked).**
This road has fast traffic and no break down lane. Although this road has a couple of quick hills, the long descent that follows makes them inconsequential.

43.9   **Left on Wilson Crossing Road by a pretty little colonial church.**

44.6   **At stop sign, turn right on Spofford Road.**
This is the best downhill section of the tour. Ahhh! The uphill on the other side is manageable.

46.6   **Right at stop sign/T-intersection on Bypass 28.**
This is a busy road with fast-moving traffic and no shoulder.

48.6   **Right into Massabesic Lake picnic area where you began.**

24 AUBURN–CANDIA

19.7 miles
Challenging—rolling with several short
hills, and three long, steady climbs

L ocated just a few miles east of Manchester, Auburn's wooded slopes, green fields, sparkling waters, and charming scenery, make it one of the most attractive rural towns in the Granite State. Surrounded on three sides by hills, the town wraps around Massabesic Lake. The lake was named by the Indian tribes who frequented its shores and crossed over its shimmering waters. Massabesic means "place of much water."

Despite Auburn's rapid growth in the last 10 years, it's retained the ambiance of a small New England agricultural town—and is a discovered jewel for cyclists.

Auburn is proudly protective of the two loon pairs which nest each spring on Massabesic Lake. Usually a lake the size of Massabesic is inadequate to support more than one pair of loons, as they often need as much as 200 acres of wetlands for their territory, but Massabesic Lake's many inlets, coves, and islands are well-suited to accommodate more than one pair.

Because the lake supplies water for nearby Manchester, the city's Water Works Department forbids swimming, skiing, or wading. But that doesn't detract from Massabesic's popularity. It's still a favorite picnic, fishing, and sailing spot.

The tour leaves from a waterfront picnic area adjacent to

Massabesic Yacht Club. An extremely popular club that boasts a two-year waiting list, Massabesic Yacht Club sponsors regattas Sunday afternoons in the summer.

Route 121, which wends its way for several miles around the lake, is a curvy, hilly road. As it enters Auburn village, it passes a magnificent Victorian home on the corner. Constructed many years ago by a Manchester contractor, it was built, records show, in one day.

Near this house is the Griffin Mill site, a shaded, grassy area by a shallow dam. The original function of the dam was to turn a unique spiral-vent water wheel for the Clark's Saw Mill and later for a grist mill that existed from 1796 onward until it burned down in 1839, never to be rebuilt.

Soon you'll cruise along Chester Turnpike, a tree-shaded road with long descents. It holds historical significance for Auburn. In 1804 Chester Turnpike became a toll road for those passing through by stagecoach from Concord to points south or east to coastal towns. There were restrictions on who was charged—no toll was to be extracted from those going to meetings, funerals, or mills. Soldiers journeying to military duty were also exempt. The fee for those not exempt was two cents—for teams and loaded vehicles.

Pedaling through the village, you'll soon encounter Bunker Hill Road. Named after the historic Boston event, it's potentially historic for you, too, as it's an accomplishment to conquer. But it's worth all the effort for the long descent that follows.

Shortly after you turn on Bunker Hill Road, you pass one of the old former taverns in town, a stopover for weary travelers who used to travel by stagecoach.

Then you're pedaling along Spofford Road, a tree-lined road in an attractive residential area. A long curving hill is the best feature of this road. It's downhill! Enjoy the ride.

RIDE INFORMATION

Highlights: Scenic lake, pond, and stream views. Historic buildings, stagecoach trail, and cooper shop.

Start: Exit 1 (Auburn/Hooksett) on Route 101E just east of Manchester. Turn south toward the traffic circle. Travel a block to the rotary, go half way around, take Bypass 28 South. Turn left into the Lake Massabesic picnic/parking area—open from 8 a.m. to 8 p.m. You can also park across the street by the softball fields.

RIDE DIRECTIONS

0.0 **Right out of parking area, a quarter of the way around the circle, then right on Route 121E.**

On the left, at about the 1.2 mile-point is The Smith House. A former summer hotel, the house is still owned and lived in by descendants of the original family. This long, white house with its expansive porch dates back to 1835. Notice the small-scale church on the lawn, complete with stained glass windows.

2.9 **Left on Hooksett Road after you cross the bridge.**
Auburn Supermarket is at this corner.

This corner is also the site of the aforementioned Victorian home that was built in a day.

A tenth of a mile down Hooksett Road on the left is the Griffin Mill. A scenic area with a waterfall, it's perfect for a picnic. Across the street from the mill site is the Griffin Public Library and Museum, which houses Indian relics, antiques, mementos and thousands of books donated in 1893 by a town founder. The library's hours vary, so if you want to see the museum, call ahead (603 483-5374).

4.4 **Right on Old Candia Road.**

5.9   Right on Chester Turnpike.

This is an attractive, tree-lined road with rock walls, burbling streams, and virtually no traffic.

8.2   Stop sign. Right on Coleman Road (becomes Eaton Road).

Coleman Road has a long, uphill climb. Directly ahead of you at this intersection is a small, red building. It's an old cooper shop. Barrelmaking was an early industry in Auburn. This same intersection is where the old toll house for Chester Turnpike was located. The building no longer exists.

Across the road from the cooper shop is the former Clay's Tavern. Built in 1750, it catered to the freighters who drove their sleds from Vermont to Massachusetts. Auburn old-timers recall seeing caravans of 50 sleds—each loaded with butter, cheese, grain, and carcasses of slaughtered hogs—making their slow journey southward. It is reported that while the 50 travelers had hearty meals and retired to the attic to sleep, the stable boys tended to the guests' hundred horses in the barn.

9.8   At the yield sign, bear left on Raymond Road.

10.2   Left at stop sign on Route 121S, through Auburn village.

10.8   Left on Bunker Hill Road.

Soon you'll begin a half-mile ascent. Hey don't complain—you get to glide down the other side.

On the left shortly after you turn on Bunker Hill Road, is a long, beige-colored house set back from the road. Another former summer hotel, called Bay View House.

At the top of Bunker Hill Road is a beautiful view of the valley. Long expanses of open field draw

Auburn-Candia

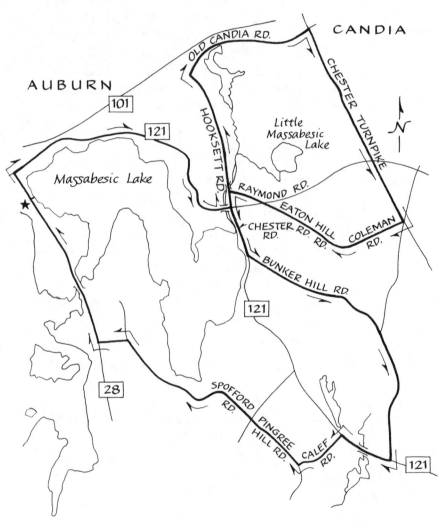

your eye to the stocked fish pond below.

Also at the intersection of Bunker Hill Road and Dearborn (at about 12.5 miles)—on the left—is a former colonial schoolhouse, now converted to a residence.

13.9   **Right at the stop sign on Chester Road (Route 121), a road with fast traffic, and no shoulder.**

14.5   **Left on Calef Road.**

15.0   **At stop sign/T-intersection, right on Pingree Hill Road (unmarked).**

15.7   **At four-way stop continue straight—on Spofford Road.**
This is the best downhill section on the tour—a curvy, hilly road. Ahhh!

17.8   **Right at stop sign on Bypass 28 (unmarked). Caution: busy road with fast traffic.**

19.7   **Turn right into the Massabesic Lake picnic area where your trip began.**

25 LONDONDERRY

25.0 miles
Moderately difficult,
with several long hills

Fragrant apple orchards in soldier-like rows present a burst of soft pink blossoms in late spring. Come fall, the trees are laden with the glistening red fruit that's America's favorite. Londonderry, a southern New Hampshire bed-room community for many Boston commuters, is home to over 1,000 acres of apple orchards and farmland.

Despite its growth in the last decade and its proximity to Route 93 and Massachusetts, Londonderry still offers re-mote, tree-shaded backroads perfect for cycling. It still exudes a strong sense of community. And it's still fiercely proud of its own slice of history.

The ride which begins in a busy area of Londonderry, soon travels along quiet country roads with rich, lush countryside accented with fine old homes, scenic lanes, and inviting solitude. Soon you pedal by the Presbyterian Church, a simple, white-spired structure with an arched stained glass window built in 1837. It's purported to be the oldest continuing Presbyterian church of its kind in all of New England. Nearby is Londonderry's second oldest church, the United Methodist Church, another shining example of the timelessness of simple elegance in colonial architecture.

If your timing's right, you may want to join in the fun for Old Home Day each August. Let the parade with marching bands, a road race, booths, and fireworks spice up your summer. (Check exact date by calling 603 434-7438.)

The quiet country roads on this ride offer endless exploring for all cycling abilities. Relax and enjoy it. Go at your own pace. And most of all, have fun!

RIDE INFORMATION

Highlights: Old cemetery, apple orchards, a huge pumpkin patch, colonial churches, pretty scenery.

Start: Park in the New Hampshire Park and Ride lot in Londonderry. Take Londonderry exit 4 off I-93. Go west on Route 102 for about a quarter of a mile. Follow signs for Park and Ride. It's located behind Wendy's Restaurant.

RIDE DIRECTIONS

0.0   Left out of parking lot to stop sign. Then left for 0.1 mile to Route 102 stop light. Right on Route 102.

0.3   At stop light, turn right on Gilcreast Road.

1.1   At stop sign, go straight on Pillsbury Road.

1.2   At stop sign, turn left on Pillsbury Road.
Weathered burying grounds appears on your left soon after turning on this road.

2.3   At stop light, turn left on Mammoth Road/Route 128. This road has a nice shoulder.
At this crossroads stands the United Methodist Church, and the Presbyterian Church. Also here, across the street, a cannon monument honors Londonderry's veterans.

If the season's right, at 2.6 miles look to your right—beyond the apple orchards—such a wonderful pumpkin patch, even the Great Pumpkin dutifully stops here on his yearly rounds!

Again if the season's right, plan to stop at Mack's apples at about the 2.8-mile mark. The cider is fresh-squeezed here and soooo good! They sell a variety of scrumptious apples, fresh fruit pies, seasonal produce, and ice cream in the summer.

3.0   **Right on Adams Road.**

3.5   **Left on Cross Road.**

4.2   **At T, go right on Young Road.**

C8C8C8

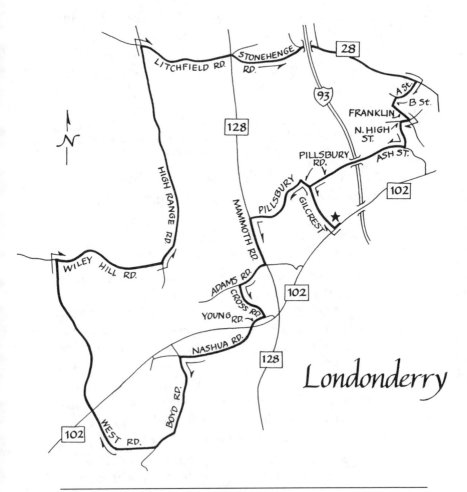

4.5   At stop sign, cross busy Route 102 to Nashua Road.

5.8   Left on Boyd Road.

7.6   At stop sign/T, turn right on West Road (un-marked).

8.5   At stop sign/blinking light, cross Route 102, still on West Road.

11.0   At stop sign T, turn right on Wiley Hill Road.
       There's a reason for the word "hill" in this road's name!

12.8   At stop sign, left on High Range Road.

13.1   At stop sign, turn left—still on High Range Road.

16.3   At stop sign, turn right on Litchfield Road.

17.7   At stop sign/red blinker, cross Route 128 to Stonehenge Road.
       A long uphill awaits you on this road.

19.2   At stop sign, turn right on Route 28 (unmarked).
       This is a busy road with no shoulder.

20.9   Right on A Street.

21.2   Left on B Street. Then at T, turn left on Franklin Street (unmarked).

21.7   Right on North High Street.

22.3   At stop sign, turn right on Ash Street for a short way to another stop sign. Left, still on Ash Street, to become Pillsbury Road.

23.9   At stop sign T, turn left on Gilcreast Road.

24.5   Left by the granite lamp post. You'll come to a stop sign. Go right, then immediate left, through an-other stop sign, and continue straight—back to the park & ride. (What you're doing here is going through the parking lot of a professional park back to your parked car.)

25.0   Back at parking lot.

26 CHESTER–SANDOWN

26.2 miles
Pleasantly rolling
with two, long, moderate hills

M any years ago Chester and Sandown were bustling, hurried, small towns that catered to people passing through by stagecoach, sled, or horseback to Haverhill, Massachusetts. Today these two sleepy communities are home to those who prefer a lifestyle that's neither bustling nor hurried. Historic New Hampshire at its best, Chester and Sandown are easily missed as vacationers clog I-93 on their way to the White Mountains or the lakes region. Fortunately, this leaves secondary roads to the east of I-93 virtually untraveled and perfect for cycling.

The tour starts in Chester—boyhood summer home of sculptor Daniel Chester French. When he was a young'n and nearby, he'd hear the resonant gong of the Chester Congregational Church bell toll the hour. Just as it still does today. Perhaps your timing will be right and you'll hear it, too.

The tour heads south through a corner of Derry, the birthplace of America's first man in space, astronaut Alan Shepard, and the site of the Robert Frost Farm, and the Taylor Up-and-Down Sawmill. Although the tour doesn't pass by these points of interest, you may want to set time aside to explore them afterward.

Soon you'll pass Sandown's Old Meeting House (circa 1774), which is credited by many as the finest meeting house in New Hampshire, some say the finest in America. Historians have lavish praise for its purity of design. Its excellent example of the skill of colonial craftspeople has earned it a place on the National Register of Historic Buildings.

Also on the National Register of Historic Places is the nearby Sandown Depot Railroad Museum. This now-inactive railroad depot contains railroad memorabilia, an antique telegraph, a velocipede, old photos, maps, and books.

The ride through the Sandown countryside is fabulous cycling! You'll glide past cozy farm houses, skirt open fields, ascend gentle hills, and glimpse horses silhouetted on distant knolls.

Heading west, you'll return to Chester. Chester Village is colonial New England at its very best. All the ingredients are there—the classic white New England Congregational Church on the corner across from the stonewall-enclosed burying grounds where monuments by famous stone masons stand quietly, a wide main street with well-kept Federal-style and Victorian homes with massive oak and chestnut trees gracing the lawns, a war memorial and cannon in Chester Square, and of course, the colonial Town Hall with Palladian windows.

RIDE INFORMATION

Highlights: Several buildings and a cemetery which are in the National Register of Historic Places, numerous summer homes of the Vanderbilts and Frenchs.

Start: The tour begins in Chester center on Route 121. Find a parking place by the post office, town hall, or Chester Library.

RIDE DIRECTIONS

0.0 **Right out of the post office parking lot on Route 121 to the stop sign at Route 102. Go right on Route 102. Note: This is a busy road with fast traffic, but**

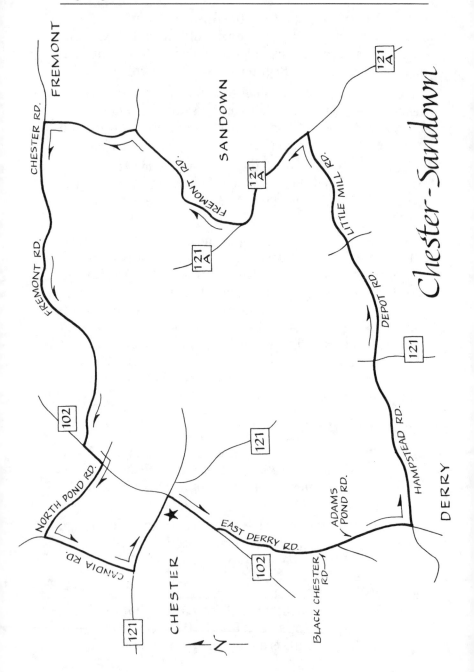

Chester-Sandown

it has a wide breakdown lane.

Shortly after this turn there's a long, uphill climb.

1.3   Left on East Derry Road (becomes Back Chester Road).

2.9   At stop sign, go left on Old Auburn Road (becomes Adams Pond Road).

4.6   At stop sign/blinking light, turn left on Hampstead Road (unmarked).

This is a moderately busy road with no shoulder.

7.5   At stop sign and blinking light, cross Route 121 (unmarked), to Depot Road.

8.8   At stop sign—continue straight—now on Little Mill Road.

10.5   Left on Main St. (Rte. 121A) to begin long uphill grade, with a long descent. A very busy road.

12.3   Bear right on Fremont Road (11 o'clock position).

This curvy, rolling road is wonderful for cycling and has very little traffic.

On your right as you make the turn is the Sandown Depot Railroad Museum (603 887-4621). On the National Register of Historic Places, the hours are Sunday 2–4 p.m.

The Old Meeting House is on the right shortly after you turn on Fremont Road. Note the Palladian window on the north side of the Old Meeting House. To tour this building, call 603 887-3946.

Notice also the Old Town Pound on your left immediately after the Old Meeting House. Stray cattle were often rounded up and temporarily kept here.

15.4   At Y, go right—still on Fremont. (A sign on the left at this intersection says North Rd., which is the road to the left). Several apartment houses will be on your left after your right turn on Fremont Rd.

16.3   **Left on Chester Road. This road becomes Fremont Road in Chester.**

There's little traffic on this road. You pedal past some weathered barns, sagging silos, and gracious farm houses. Immense, stately maples dignify front lawns while horses and Hereford cattle graze nearby.

21.4   **At stop sign, turn left on Route 102 (unmarked). This road has moderate volume, fast-paced traffic, and a wide shoulder.**

22.2   **Right on North Pond Road.**

23.8   **Left at stop sign on Candia Road.**

24.8   **At stop sign, turn left on Route 121 toward Chester center. It's uphill into Chester.**

As you enter Chester, on the left you'll notice a small brick building. Now a residence, it used to be Chester's schoolhouse.

Also on your left shortly after the schoolhouse, is a large barn with an ell on the right side. It has a cupola with a weathervane. It is the former Elliot Tavern, built in 1747.

Closer to the center of town, also on the left, is the Richardson-French house, a cream-colored structure with white trim and double chimneys. The French family are long-time residents of Chester. Sculptor Daniel Chester French, best known for his heroic-sized statue of Abraham Lincoln which resides in the Lincoln Memorial in Washington, D.C., used to summer here with his grandfather. French was not given a middle name, and later chose Chester because of his fond memories of Chester, New Hampshire.

Adjacent and to the right of the Richardson-French house is the French-Dexter House, a pristine white building with Federal-style architecture, complete with formal sunken gardens on the grounds.

Across the street from these two houses on your right at about 25.6 miles is the Vanderbilt house. Somewhat obscured by trees, it too is a formal Federal-style structure with shutters, double chimney and a small portico. A unique feature of this home is its eyebrow dormer.

Other noteworthy structures grace this small town. Don't miss the Crawford House (a sign identifies it) on the left, nor the stately Aikin house (on left), a formal Federal-style home painted yellow and surrounded by an imposing white fence. The Congregational Church and the burying grounds across the street are in the National Register of Historic Places.

The houses mentioned here are all private homes and are not open to the public.

26.2   The post office and town hall are on your right.

27 SALEM-HAMPSTEAD

20.1 miles
Flat terrain; some gently, rolling hills

E ven though this ride meanders through a more densely populated area of New Hampshire, rest assured you'll still be delighted by the rural quality of this farming and residential community. Designed by one of the founders of New Hampshire's oldest and largest bike clubs, Granite State Wheelman's Dave Topham, this ride includes all the elements of a New Hampshire scenic bike tour—picturesque ponds, stretches of stone walls, cows and horses grazing in open fields, and of course, colonial churches and tree-canopied roads. Oh, and great places for food after the ride!

Beginning in Salem, the ride continues into Atkinson on the Massachusetts border, East Hampstead, to Derry and back.

Derry was the boyhood home of Cmdr. Alan Shepard, Jr., the first American in space. Also located on the outskirts of Derry is the Robert Frost Farm, where the poet lived for 11 years of his life. Restored to its turn-of-the-20th-century condition, the house contains original family furniture pieces. Displays and videotapes feature readings of Frost's work. For more information, call 603 432-3091.

North Salem is home of America's Stonehenge. You cycle past this on the tour. The attraction features prehistoric stone structures proven by carbon dating to form the oldest known megalithic site on this continent. Indications are that the site may be 4,000 years old. Worth a stop!

Of course nothing more aptly says "New Hampshire" than the great outdoors—and this trip surely will dazzle you with blazing colors if you choose to ride it in the fall. The bonus is that most of the "leaf peepers" will be up north craning their necks, and hence will leave these roads less traveled so *you* can enjoy them!

RIDE INFORMATION

Highlights: America's Stonehenge, pretty scenery, colonial churches, stone walls, upscale residential communities, and some terrific downhills!

Start: Plaza 97 on Rte. 97 in North Salem. From I-93, take exit 2 east on Main St. Go 3.6 miles to 399 Main St. Park your car in the front of the lot near the traffic light on Main St.

RIDE DIRECTIONS

0.0 **Right out of the parking lot on Hampstead Rd. (north). This road becomes Shannon Rd.**

Plaza 97 has some super places to eat. Most notably, Casa Vecchia. If you're interested in eating there, reservations are needed or you'll never get in. Also this plaza has a deli and a convenience store.

0.5 **Stay straight on what is now Shannon Rd.**

0.9 **Right on Hooker Farm Rd. (Becomes Salem Road.)**

Soon you'll see Captain's Pond on the right. This is a pastoral road complete with cows munching lazily on hay in the field. The cows near Captain's Pond have been pretty-much replaced by fancy homes—some over $1 million.

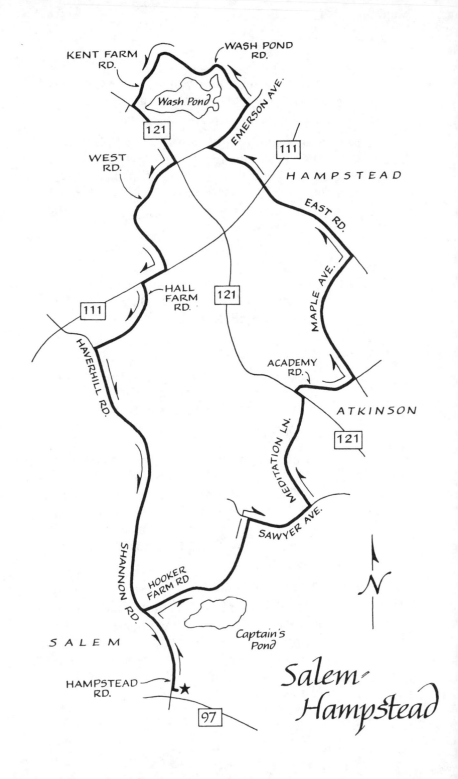

KENT FARM RD.

WASH POND RD.

Wash Pond

121

EMERSON AVE.

111

HAMPSTEAD

WEST RD.

EAST RD.

MAPLE AVE.

121

HALL FARM RD.

111

HAVERHILL RD.

ACADEMY RD.

ATKINSON

121

MEDITATION LN.

SAWYER AVE.

SHANNON RD.

HOOKER FARM RD

Captain's Pond

SALEM

N

HAMPSTEAD RD.

★

97

Salem-Hampstead

2.8 Right at T-intersection on Sawyer Ave. The signs are confusing at this intersection. But ignore them and go right.

3.2 Stay straight (still on Sawyer Ave.).

3.5 Left on Meditation Lane.

4.6 At stop sign, left on Rte. 121N.
If it's time for a cappuchino stop, do so at the Atkinson Village Store on the right at this turn.

4.65 Right on Academy Road.

5.2 Left on Maple Ave. Shift down for a brief climb, then enjoy the downhills on this road.

6.8 At stop sign/T-intersection, go left on East Rd. (unmarked).

8.1 Cross Rte. 111. Be careful! Stay on East Rd.

8.9 Right on Emerson Ave. Busy road. Be careful.

9.5 Left on Wash Pond Rd.

11.1 At stop sign, go straight on Kent Farm Rd. (unmarked).

11.7 At stop sign/T-intersection, go left on Rte. 121S (unmarked) into Hampstead.
Hampstead Center Market is here in case it's time for an ice cream stop.

12.6 Right on West Road.
Congratulations—you've earned a couple of nice, long downhills! Enjoy the ride!

14.3 At stop sign, go right on Rte. 111 (unmarked).

14.7 Left on Hall Farm Rd. (Changes to Klein Dr.)
A Dunkin Donuts and a convenience store are at this corner.

15.5 Left on Haverhill Rd.
At 15.9 miles is America's Stonehenge.

17.0 Stay straight on Shannon Rd. (unmarked).

19.5   **Stay straight—road becomes Hampstead Rd.**

20.1   **Left into Plaza 97 parking lot.**

28 WINDHAM–SALEM

38.2 miles
Rolling, several uphill climbs. One long
climb. Seven miles of this ride are on
busy roads. Not a good ride for children.

This ride threads its way through part of the proverbial southern tier—the "boom towns" of 1980s overdevelopment fame. But for most of the ride, you'll be hard pressed to believe you're so near the Massachusetts border. And well it should be that way—this is a pleasure ride!

You travel through Windham, Pelham, and Salem—bedroom communities for Massachusetts commuters. But all offer their own unusual features. Your ride begins near Windham common—a compact area dominated by the library, fire station, and town hall. The white, fieldstone, and green-shuttered structures nestle together as perfectly as any New England setting ever dreamed up by Paramount Pictures.

Windham is also home to the Searles Castle. Edward Francis Searles, born in 1841, is remembered as an eccentric, lonely man who compulsively acquired property, constructed buildings and then lost interest in them soon after their completion. The castle, surrounded by miles of stone walls, is worth a look. A short side trip on this ride brings you to the castle's gate.

Pelham offers quiet countryside and migrant apple pickers who wave and flash big smiles as you cruise through the orchard during apple-picking season. Its backroads also provide some challenging climbs—what's low gear for, folks?

The Salem component of the ride takes you past Canobie Lake Park—an amusement park that first opened in 1902— where high-tech thrills are combined with lake cruises, live shows, dining. Fun for the whole family. For more information, call 603 893-3506.

You might want to schedule a side trip to the number one tourist attraction in New Hampshire—Rockingham Park in Salem. Over a million people visit this pari-mutuel horse racing track annually. For additional information, call 603 898-2311.

Another jog in your itinerary and you'll be at America's Stonehenge—a prehistoric stone structure (proven by carbon dating) to be the oldest known megalithic site on the continent. Research indicates that the site may be 4,000 years old. Deciphered inscriptions offer evidence that Celt-Iberians lived here 800–300 B.C.

RIDE INFORMATION

Highlights: Scenic and sweet-scented ride past an apple orchard, Canobie Lake Park, Searles Castle, photo opportunities.

Start: Park and Ride lot on Route 111 in Windham. Take Exit 3 on I-93 to Route 111W. Park and Ride is on right half a mile from exit.

RIDE DIRECTIONS

0.0 **Right out of parking lot on Route 111W.**

0.5 **Shortly after stop light, turn right on Church Road.**
A park with benches, gazebo, and walking bridge over a stream here invite you to stop a spell.

0.6 **At stop sign/T-intersection across from fire station, go right on North Lowell Road.**

The Windham Presbyterian Church, built by early Scottish settlers, and the town hall are on your right.

2.5   Left on East Nashua Road.

2.8   Right on Beacon Hill Road.

4.3   At T, go right on Fordway Extension (unmarked).

Beware of moose!

5.5   At stop sign, go left on Kendall Pond Road.

6.5   Stop sign. Continue straight on South Road.
      At about 7.9 miles (by bridge on right) ducks
      paddle about in a small stream. Good place for a
      break.

7.9   At Y, bear right.

8.0   At stop sign/T-intersection, go left—still on South
      Road (unmarked).

9.5   At stop sign, cross Mammoth Road (unmarked),
      then turn left on Griffin Road.

11.6   Right on Robinson Road.

14.0   Left on Old Derry Road by Hudson Speedway.
      Don't miss the working Holstein farm along this
      road. If your timing's right—early spring—you
      may catch the sweet smell of silage.

15.5   Left on Greeley Street.

16.9   Right on Highland Street.

18.0   Left on George Street.

18.2   At stop sign, take a quick left jog, then right on
      Adelaide Street.

18.8   At stop sign/T-intersection, go right on Route 111
      (unmarked), then immediate left on Melendy Road.

19.4   At stop sign, stay straight—still on Melendy.

19.9   At stop sign T, left on Pelham Road (unmarked).

21.0   At T yield sign, turn right on Bush Hill Road.
      Begin a mile-long climb. The terrain is hilly for
      the next four miles. There's an interesting Tudor
      country home with a white gazebo in the middle
      of a pond on this road. A Conestoga wagon with
      a small herd of faithful horses, makes its way
      across the harsh plain here.

21.1   Stay straight—don't go right on Wason Road.
      At about 22.0 miles at the crest of the hill is an

apple orchard, look right for a nice view of distant mountains. Great road!

24.8   **At yield sign, turn right on Mammoth Road (unmarked), then an immediate left on Burns Road (unmarked, a low stone wall is a landmark).**

25.7   **At stop sign T, go right on Route 111A (unmarked).** Pelham High School is at this intersection.

௫௫௫

25.9   Left on Willow Street.

26.7   **At stop light, turn left on Route 38N (unmarked).
        Caution: This is a very busy road with no shoulder.**
        There are several stop lights along this stretch.
        Also, lots of places to eat.

32.9   **At stop light, turn left on South Policy Street.
        Caution: Lots of traffic.**
        No shoulder for a mile, then a wide one.

34.1   **Stop light, go straight on North Policy Road. Busy
        road, but traffic is not fast-paced.**
        Canobie Park is on this road.

36.0   **At stop sign, turn left on Route 111W. Much fast
        traffic.**
        Around 36.5 miles, look to right to see rock walls
        and road to Searles Castle. (It may be difficult to
        see through the vegetation during the summer.)

36.8   **At Y stop light, turn right, still on Route 111.**

38.2   **Right into park & ride parking lot.**

SEACOAST REGION

29 ROCHESTER-LEBANON, ME

26.5 miles
Mostly flat, some rolling hills

Near the Maine border, the quiet, rural community of Rochester, NH, was incorporated in 1722. Back then 60,000 acres of forested land was about all there was to Rochester. Soon immigrants arrived and the complexion of the landscape began to change as farmers carved out homesteads, developed roads, and built mills. Railroads hit this area in the mid-1800s, and Rochester became the transportation hub of New Hampshire's Seacoast. Traditional manufacturing of products also expanded during this time, producing such items as shoes, woolens, and bricks. Today the city's largest employer is Cabletron Systems, Inc., with 2,500 employees.

Rochester is also a hidden jewel for cyclists. This ride quickly takes you out of town and soon such delightful sights as stone walls, white-paddock fences with horses grazing beyond, old burying grounds, picture-perfect maples, and white colonial churches, will greet you as you skirt into southern Maine.

During the fall foliage season, this ride is particularly enjoyable as the trees change color and present their last-hurrah of dying colors—flaming oranges, brilliant yellows, near-neon reds, and subdued russets. Don't miss it!

RIDE INFORMATION

Highlights: Pretty countryside riding. Nice scenery—horses grazing, maples gracefully overhanging the road, weathered burial grounds, stone walls.

Start: Rich's Shopping Plaza, Rte. 11, Rochester. Take exit 14 off the Spaulding Tnpk. At end of ramp, take right to next stop sign. Take right again. At lights, right into shopping plaza.

RIDE DIRECTIONS

0.0 Right at lights on Rte. 11, leaving shopping plaza.

0.4 Left on Dewey Street to end.

0.8 Cross foot bridge over Cocheco River.

1.0 When you see the "Do Not Enter" sign, go right. You are in the Spaulding High School parking lot.

1.1 At yield sign, bear right onto road.

1.3 At lights, go left on Rte. 125S.

1.5 At lights, go left across railroad crossing on Summer St. (unmarked). Salvation Army is on your right at this turn.

1.7 Follow one-way signs to Rte. 202/11.

1.8 Right on Rte. 202/11 (Eastern Ave.)

3.1 At light, right on Rte. 202E.

3.2 At light, left on Salmon Falls Road.

4.7 Right on Flat Rock Bridge Road.

5.2 At stop sign, left on River Road.

6.6 Right on North Rochester Road (unmarked).
Maples drape this road in all their splendid fall glory (provided you're cycling in the fall, and you *should* be!). Birch interspersed in the landscape add to the serene beauty of the season.

8.2 At stop sign, left on Shapleigh Road.

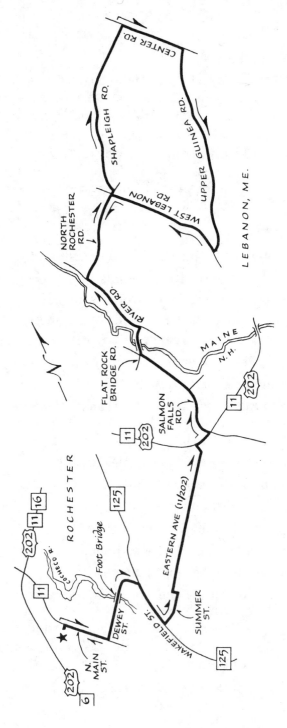

Rochester~Lebanon, ME

11.3   At stop sign/T-intersection, right on Center Road (unmarked).

   Faraway mountain vistas, panoramic fall foliage, and picturesque white colonial churches, make this road delightful.

12.5   Right on Upper Guinea Road.

16.0   At stop sign/T-intersection, right on West Lebanon Road (unmarked).

18.3   At stop sign, left on North Rochester Road.

19.9   At stop sign/T-intersection, go left on River Road (unmarked). You are now retracing your steps back to the start of the ride.

21.3   Right on Flat Rock Bridge Road.

21.8   At stop sign, left on Salmon Falls Road (unmarked). This road has fast traffic.

23.2   Right on Rte. 202 at the light.

23.4   Left on Rte. 202/11 (Eastern Ave.) to stop sign. Then left half a block to stop sign.

24.8   At stop sign, right on Summer Street.

25.0   Right on Rte. 125N at lights (by railroad crossing).

25.2   Right on Rte. 125 at lights (onto Wakefield St.)

25.3   Bear left at yield sign into Spaulding H.S. parking lot.

25.5   Left at the stop sign in the school parking lot.

25.7   Cross the foot bridge, and continue on Dewey St.

26.0   Right on Main St. (Rte. 11).

26.5   Left at lights into parking lot of shopping plaza.

30 ROCHESTER–DOVER

15.6 miles
Rolling, a few small hills, one long hill,
a good family ride. (Walk bikes up hills
that are too difficult for a child.)

Nestled between the Cocheco and Salmon Falls rivers in northeastern Strafford County, Rochester and Dover are close to the beaches, Lakes Region, and the White Mountains. Even though they're off the beaten path, both of these small towns have pockets of congested traffic. The beauty of this ride is that you only skirt the edges of these thriving mini-metropolises.

Known as the "Lilac City" because of the profusion of this fragrant shrub, Rochester was incorporated in 1722 as Norway Plains, later to be called Rochester. In the early 19th century Rochester sprouted factories along the Salmon Falls River, where boots, shoes, woolen goods, bricks, and pottery were produced.

Dover is even older than Rochester. In fact, it's considered to be the oldest permanent settlement in the state, founded in 1623 by fishermen and traders who navigated the waters of the Great Bay area. Eventually the Cocheco Fall's waterpower was harnessed by industries such as grist mills, cotton mills, and saw mills. Today many of the same brick mill buildings that supported the early industries have been renovated, and once again house businesses, but on a smaller scale. The mill buildings blend comfortably with other architectural styles prevalent in the area, especially colonial and Victorian.

From late June to early September, Dover celebrates the Cocheco Arts Festival (603 742-2218). Held in the old mill complex beside the Cocheco River, the festival features children's concerts and programs, as well as concerts for adults by regional performers.

CACACA

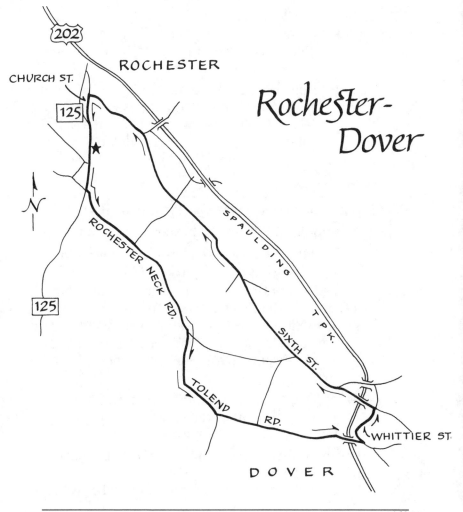

Despite its proximity to Dover and Rochester, this ride is country all the way—and very pretty country, at that. Small cemeteries with granite slab walls. Rolling farmland with hay bales smelling of freshly cut alfalfa. Stone walls. Wild clover and corn waving in the breeze.

It's classic backroads New Hampshire. Bring the kids, a picnic lunch, an adventurous attitude, and have a great day!

RIDE INFORMATION

Highlights: Scenic, rolling farmland. Easy enough for older children—just a little hilly, minimal traffic, a fairly short ride.

Start: Gonic Plaza on Route 125. It's 3.5 miles beyond the Route 9/125 intersection on the left as you're heading north. (At the 9/125 intersection, don't miss Calef's Country Store—it's worth the stop. Great cheeses!)

RIDE DIRECTIONS

0.0 Right out of Gonic Plaza parking lot on Route 125.

0.5 At stop light, left on Rochester Neck Road.

4.0 At T intersection (with a chain-link fence ahead of you), turn left on Tolend Road (unmarked).

7.3 Immediately after crossing a bridge, take a sharp left on Whittier Street. Right after you make this turn, you'll see a bus-stop shelter on left.

For refreshments, Dicicco's Market is at this turn. You'll encounter a steep uphill climb on this road.

7.8 At stop sign/red blinker, left on Sixth Street.

This road has little traffic. At 13.7 miles on the right is a Pick-Your-Own Berries farm.

14.6 Left on Church Street in Gonic. (Just before the post office.)

If you're starving, Corona Pizza and Sylvain's

Groceries are at this turn.

The small village of Gonic has a pretty little white-clapboard colonial Baptist church with stained glass windows.

15.1   **At stop sign, left on Route 125S.**
Caution: storm grates.

15.6   **Right to Gonic Plaza.**

31 LEE–CENTER BARNSTEAD

64.2 miles
Rolling, hilly, two mile-looong hills

This tour passes through open country with expansive pastures, classic New England barns, houses dating from the 1700s and 1800s, photo-perfect birch stands, and grazing cows and horses. The ride takes in lots of scenery and lots of miles—it's a trip for hardier riders.

The ride begins in the quiet, country town of Lee, then meanders through Madbury, Barrington, Strafford, Barnstead, Pittsfield, Northwood, Nottingham, and back to Lee.

If you plan it just right, you can catch the Pittsfield Rotary Clubs Annual Hot Air Balloon Festival the last weekend in July, where 20+ hot air balloons take flight over the picturesque Suncook Valley. Craft booths, lots of food, entertainment, and an overwhelming supply of town pride are evident at this event.

At about halfway you pedal along deserted roads that lead to Center Barnstead. A cozy, small town, Center Barnstead has its own points of pride—like the pretty Christian Church with colonial appointments, a clock tower, and weather vane. And then there's the gazebo, the weathered war monument on the expansive green, and the well-kept burial grounds.

Those who love antiques will be in their glory on this ride. You travel through Northwood—the mecca of New Hampshire "antiquedom." Whatever you could possibly desire is available—furniture, Depression glass, books, antique shawls and hats, tools—it's all here.

RIDE INFORMATION

Highlights: Historic Calef's Country Store, post card New England villages, historic buildings, water views, great for fall cycling.

Lodging: If you want to make this a weekend tour, there are several options for accommodations. The night before the ride, you could stay in Durham at the Hannah House Bed and Breakfast (603 659-5500). A non-smoking inn, it offers a cozy, country atmosphere. Also in Durham is the Hickory Pond Inn (603 659-2227). If you want to stay overnight halfway through the tour, consider the Appleview Orchard Bed and Breakfast in Pittsfield (603 435-6867).

Start: Take Route 125N to Route 155N to Lee center. Park by the Lee Public Library and Lee Police Department. If you intend to make this an overnight trip, let the Lee Police Department know you're leaving your car.

RIDE DIRECTIONS

0.0 Left out of the Lee Police Department parking lot on to Route 155N. This road has moderate traffic.

1.7 Left still on Route 155N.

7.9 At stop light, left on Route 9W.
This road has a wide shoulder.

14.0 At stop light at Route 125/9, go straight across— still on Route 9W.

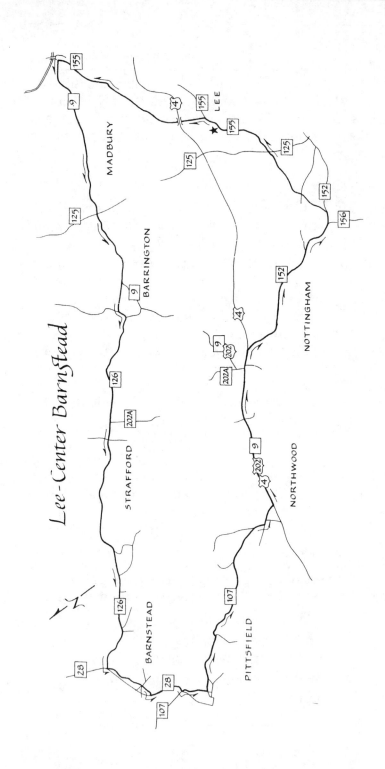

Lee-Center Barnstead

On your left at this corner is Calef's Country Store. For over a century, they've sold hundreds of gallons of maple syrup, barrels of pickles, and tons of "they'll come for miles around" Cheddar cheese (in a variety of flavors). Calef's was for many years home to the Barrington Post Office and Fire Department. The semi-professional Barrington Orioles used to play baseball in the field out back. The store has seen six generations of the Calef family.

16.8 **At Y, bear right on Route 126N.**
This road has no shoulder and little traffic.

18.1 **At T stop sign, left on Route 126/202W for 0.2 mile.**

18.3 **Right on 126N.**
At 21.2 miles there's a half-mile uphill made bearable by panoramic views at its crest.

22.4 **At T stop sign, left on Route 126N. At this turn, directly ahead of you is the Strafford Historical Society.**
The historical society is open from 1-4 p.m. Saturdays in July and August.

Soon on the right is the Military Academy, where the New Hampshire National Guard train. After the Academy, you begin a long, serious climb.

You'll catch panoramic mountain views along Route 126.

Entering Barnstead with its old burial grounds, and white colonial churches with a clock tower or bell, you'll have the perfect fodder for classic New England photo opportunities. A bit farther brings you to Center Barnstead where the village common sports a gazebo, a war monument, and an opportunity to relax for lunch on the shaded green.

For refreshments, stop at Mountain's General Store in town. A fascinating old country store, you'll find unexpected pleasures—everything from homemade root beer and assorted candies to antiques and collectibles. Refuel with pizza, a calzone, or something from the deli.

32.4   **Just before stop sign/red blinker, turn left toward Barnstead Parade.**

34.4   **At stop sign, left on Route 28S.**

35.3   **Right toward Route 107.**

36.0   **At stop sign, cross Route 28—still on Route 107S.** This is a busy intersection, walk your bike.

Very near here is Appleview Orchard Bed and Breakfast (603 435-6867) in Pittsfield.

36.8   **Left in center of Pittsfield, still on Route 107S.** Near this intersection is a super market for a food stop.

As you leave Pittsfield, a 1.5-mile uphill challenges you, followed by a steep descent and yet another uphill. (Hey—this is good exercise!)

44.3   **Right on Route 107S.**

44.9   **At stop sign, left on Route 4, a busy road with a wide shoulder. You are entering Northwood.** There are several places along here to eat.

51.5   **Right on Route 152E.**

57.4   **Stay left on Route 152E.**

61.0   **At stop sign/red blinker at Route 125, cross the road—staying on Route 152E.**

62.1   **Left on Route 155N.**

64.2   **Back at Lee Police Station and Town Hall where your ride began.**

32 NEWMARKET-LEE OR NEWMARKET-DURHAM

17.9 or 23.9 miles
Rolling, a few short hills

Perhaps this ride should have been called "The Agricultural Tour." You will be cruising past working farms that have a variety of cows—Guernseys, Holsteins, Angus—and pigs, chickens, sheep, horses... And fields of corn, pumpkins, etc. Oh, did I say this is near the University of New Hampshire's Durham campus and some of these farms are designed for students who are studying the business of farming?

Even if farms aren't your favorite attraction, this ride is a winner because of the relaxing roads you're pedaling on. Tree-lined routes, serene ponds with wildlife, picturesque farm scenes with massive maples in the back yard, stone walls, and rolling meadows, make for a great ride.

You get two tours for the price of one in this chapter. You can choose to go 17.9 miles or 23.9 miles. Both are great rides for the fall foliage season. Lots of hardwood trees to show off New Hampshire's splendid fall wardrobe.

Newmarket is an old mill town which has undergone quite a bit of growth of late, and even the once unattractive old mill buildings are taking on a new face as they're converted into residential condos that sport high ceilings and terrific views of the river. The town is on the Lamprey River,

Newmarket-Lee -or- Newmarket-Durham

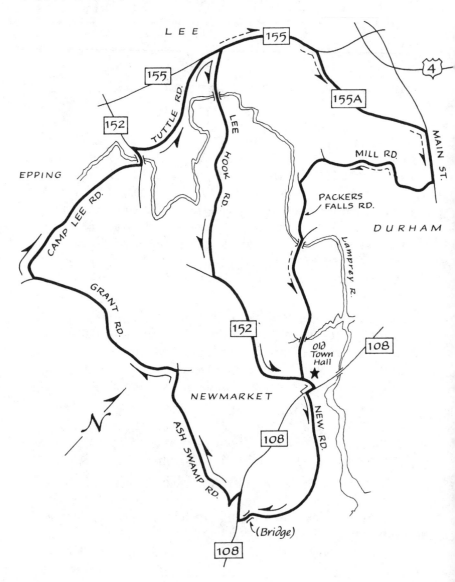

LEE

155

155

152

TUTTLE RD.

LEE HOOK RD.

155A

4

MAIN ST.

MILL RD.

EPPING

CAMP LEE RD.

GRANT RD.

152

PACKERS FALLS RD.

DURHAM

Lamprey R.

108

Old Town Hall
★

NEWMARKET

ASH SWAMP RD.

108

NEW RD.

(Bridge)

108

N

which empties into Great Bay—a natural estuary, where fresh and salt water meet. Nearby Moody Point offers walking trails, wildlife sightings, docks, and a pavilion perfect for a picnic lunch.

Newmarket is also home to runner Lynn Jennings, U.S. Olympic bronze medalist. Lee is a rural community that offers space to breathe and some wonderful cycling roads.

The extended tour takes you into Durham, where the University of New Hampshire is located, as well as home to the UNH Wildcat hockey teams—both women's and men's teams have impressive wins to their names. The women's team won the national NCAA championship in 1998, and both men's and women's teams were finalists for the 1999 NCAA championship games. UNH's Jason Krog was the recipient of the 1999 Hobey Baker award and he now plays for the NHL.

RIDE INFORMATION

Highlights: Both tours are really pretty rides. Stone walls, working farms, easy pedaling, nice scenery.

Start: Town hall (the big brick building) on Rte. 152 a block west of Rte. 108 in Newmarket.

RIDE DIRECTIONS

0.0 **Leave the parking lot on the road perpendicular to the town hall, past Gepetto's Pizza to the intersection of Rte. 152 and 108.**

Do stop at Gepetto's Pizza on your return. They have great pizza!

0.1 **At T intersection, go right on Rte. 108.**

0.2 **Left on New Road.**

This is a pretty, tree-lined road with ponds, and no traffic.

2.6 **At stop sign, turn right on Rte. 108.**

This is a busy road, but you'll be off it in a jiffy. The Ship to Shore Restaurant at this corner has a varied, reasonably priced menu.

3.0 **Left on Ash Swamp Road. (This is the road across from Great Bay Athletic Club, and to the left of the golf course).**

Tree-lined with stone walls and old graveyards, this road provides pleasant views and no traffic.

5.2 **At four-way stop, go left on Grant Road.**

This is another beautiful road with stone walls, rolling meadows, and an old scenic farm with a massive maple tree and white paddock fences that beg for a Kodak moment.

7.7 **Right on Camp Lee Road.**

Horses graze on a horse farm on this road—and another farm later on with chickens scratching about near the road.

10.0 **At stop sign/T intersection, go left on Rte. 152 (unmarked) and cross the bridge.**

10.1 **Right on Tuttle Road.**

Along this road are more horse farms. Also a farm with mud-loving pigs. Pumpkin and sunflower crops are also harvested here.

11.9 **At yield sign, turn right on Rte. 155 (unmarked).**

*****

Go to next page for route notes on the 23.9-mile trip.

*****

12.4 **Right on Lee Hook Road (by Jeremiah Smith Grange).**

This road passes one of the UNH agricultural farms. Farms that raise sheep and a variety of cow breeds—Angus, Holstein, Guernseys (Hey—this book is written by a South Dakota farmer's daughter who grew up around cows!)

16.0   At stop sign/T intersection, turn left on Rte. 152.

17.9   Left into town hall parking lot.

*****

Directions for the 23.9-mile trip extended trip (into Durham):

After the turn at the yield sign onto Rte. 155 at 11.9 miles, continue on Rte. 155 through Lee Center.

14.2   Bear right a bit onto Rte. 155A.

16.3   Right at stop sign on Main Street (unmarked) into Durham.

Numerous eating places abound along Main Street. The Bagelry, Breaking New Grounds, Young's Family Restaurant, pizza places and ice cream stores.

17.5   Right on Mill Road.

20.1   At stop sign T-intersection, go left on Packer's Falls Road (unmarked).

21.4   At 3-way stop sign, continue straight on Packer's Falls Road.

If you want to do a bit of antiquing, turn right here and check out Wiswall House Antiques down the road.

At 21.7 miles don't miss the singing stream where the water tumbles over the rocks creating a mini white-water area. Nice rocks for a picnic—or wade into the stream and cool off.

At 22.4 miles a classic old burying ground on your left boasts a stonework wall with horizontal slabs that are so precisely placed, it has endured hundreds of years.

23.8   At stop sign, turn left on Rte. 152.

On your right at this corner, don't miss the

Deacon Paul Chapman House. Built in 1764, this Federal-style colonial, which features a center chimney, is a fine example of a well-preserved historic structure.

23.9   Left on Beech Street extension into the town hall parking lot.

33 EXETER–DURHAM POINT

37.4 miles
Rolling, with lots of moderate hills

Exeter and Durham. These two small Seacoast towns are known for their academic institutions—Exeter for Phillips Exeter Academy and Durham for the University of New Hampshire.

Exeter, a 350-year-old New England community, is home to one of the most famous preparatory schools in the country—Phillips Exeter Academy, founded in 1783. The sprawling campus with its ivy-covered brick buildings is located in the Front Street Historic District. Here architectural design spans the gamut from historic colonial homes constructed in the 1600s and 1700s—like the Gilman Garrison House (1690) and Cincinnati Memorial Hall (1721)—to the contemporary Phillips Exeter Academy Library designed by Louis Kahn.

If you have the time and inclination, plan to take a historic walking tour of Exeter. Booklets for four self-guided tours are available from the Exeter Area Chamber of Commerce at 120 Water Street. Guided tours are also offered by the American Independence Museum, One Governors Lane.

Exeter also offers unique specialty shops—a card shop with over 3,000 cards, a collector's book store, a toy store with prices from $10 to $300. Exeter boasts some of the best restaurants around. The cuisine ranges from down-homesy

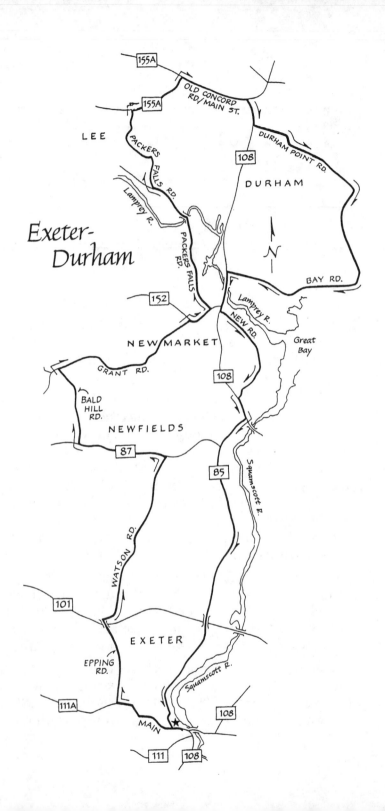

casual restaurants with steaming chowders and home-baked "Annadamma" bread, to Szechuan and international gourmet elegance.

Halfway through your ride, you enter Durham. Durham ranks among New Hampshire's oldest towns. In its colonial days, Durham was the scene of some of the worst Indian massacres in American history. Today, a calmer atmosphere prevails in this collegiate town, which harbors 12,000 University of New Hampshire students.

RIDE INFORMATION

Highlights: Several historic markers, Arabian horse farms, numerous well-kept burying grounds, a couple choice picnic spots, historic houses and walking tours, classic colonial architecture, Exeter Academy, the University of New Hampshire, and an apple orchard.

Start: In downtown Exeter park in the municipal parking lot on Water Street (the main street) by House of Travel and the Szechuan Taste.

RIDE DIRECTIONS

0.0 **Left out of parking lot on Water Street/Main St. (This becomes Epping Road, and is also Rte. 27W). Caution: railroad tracks at 0.6 mile. Stay on Rte. 27W to cross over Rte. 101.**

2.5 **Right on Watson Road. Becomes Oakland Rd.**

5.2 **At stop sign/T-intersection, go left on Route 87 (unmarked).**
On this road you pedal past towering silos, a prosperous horse farm, majestic maples, and a stately, Federal-style colonial home built in 1740.

7.2 **Right on Bald Hill Road.**
This turn is by old burying grounds, dignified with expansive maples gracing its stone wall.

8.9   **At stop sign/Y-intersection, go right on Grant Road.**

11.2   **At stop sign, go straight—still on Grant Road.**
There's an Arabian Horse Farm on this road.

12.4   **At stop sign, go right on Route 152E.**

12.9   **Left on Packer's Falls Road.**
At this turn, don't miss the historic Deacon Paul Chapman House. Built in 1764, this Federal-style colonial features a center chimney, and is a fine example of a well-preserved historic structure.

At about 15.0 miles there's a bridge over rushing water. Large rocks invite you to stop here and have a picnic lunch. Also this road boasts three old, weathered burying grounds, spreading maple trees, and a granite block wall built in the mid-1800s.

15.3   **At stop sign, stay straight. Wiswall Road on left.**

16.0   **Bear right with the curve.**

17.9   **Stop sign. Go right on Route 155A (unmarked).**

19.2   **At stop sign, turn right on Main Street (unmarked) through Durham.**
Along Durham's main street, many places are available to stop and grab a bite, or indulge in ice cream!

20.7   **Right on Route 108S. Caution: Busy intersection!**
This turn takes you past the colonial Community Church of Durham. The cupola dates back to circa 1849.

Also along this road are several historic markers. Major General John Sullivan (1740-1795), a revolutionary patriot, soldier and politician, served under Washington from Cambridge to Valley Forge. Later he served three terms as governor of New Hampshire.

The Oyster River Massacre, and the Packer's Falls historic marker are also here. The falls, a couple of miles from this point on the Lamprey River, once provided waterpower and industry for early settlers.

21.1   Left on Durham Point Road. Becomes Bay Rd.

This is a hilly, but outrageously wonderful stretch of road with fabulous views of Great Bay, occasional glimpses of Great Blue Herons fishing in the marshes, and terrific fall riding! Note at 23.7 miles on the right is an 1834 brick school house.

28.9   At stop sign, left on Rte. 108S (unmarked) through Newmarket.

Soon you pass a cluster of mill buildings in the industrial area of Newmarket, and places to eat.

29.2   Bear left, staying on Route 108S. Caution: busy road.

29.5   Left on New Road.

This is a pretty, tree-lined road with ponds, and no traffic.

31.9   Left on Rte. 108S a short way.

32.3   Right on Route 85S through Newfields, and back to Exeter. Caution: Lots of traffic.

This stretch of road has two architecturally noteworthy New England churches with such classic architectural features as Gothic stained glass windows, rose windows, and bell towers.

Newfields Country Store is on this road for a food stop.

A historic marker along this road notes the life of Brigadier General Enoch Poor. A successful merchant and ship builder, Poor served under Washington, Sullivan, and Lafayette. Congress commissioned him Brigadier General in 1777.

33.7   At Y, bear left through Swasey Parkway.

      This is a pretty place for a picnic—complete with a mesmerizing, gentle waterfall.

37.2   At stop sign, turn left on Main Street (Water Street).

37.4   **You're back at the municipal parking lot (on the right) where your ride began.**

34 KINGSTON-SANDOWN

22.4 miles
Rolling, with lots of moderate uphills

Historic rural Kingston in southern Rockingham County is an old farming community. One of the oldest New Hampshire towns (said to be fifth), Kingston's charter dates to 1694.

In the past it was a lumber town, later to become a renowned international center for its poultry business. The New Hampshire Red chicken, in demand from 1930 to 1960, was shipped to every part of the U.S., South America, and Europe.

Kingston's most famous historic figure was Declaration of Independence signer, Josiah Bartlett. Also New Hampshire's first governor, Bartlett, came to Kingston at age 21 as a physician. His house on Main Street is a National Historic Landmark and is listed on the National Register of Historic Places.

If you have time, you may want to have lunch at the historic Kingston 1686 House Restaurant. Kingston House's reputation for fine cuisine is rivaled only by its cozy atmosphere, which is enhanced by an original beehive oven, wide pine floor boards, Indian shutters, nine-over-six window panes and a pulpit staircase.

Skirting into nearby Danville and Sandown, this ride is an absolute joy in the fall. It is exquisitely breathtaking with the

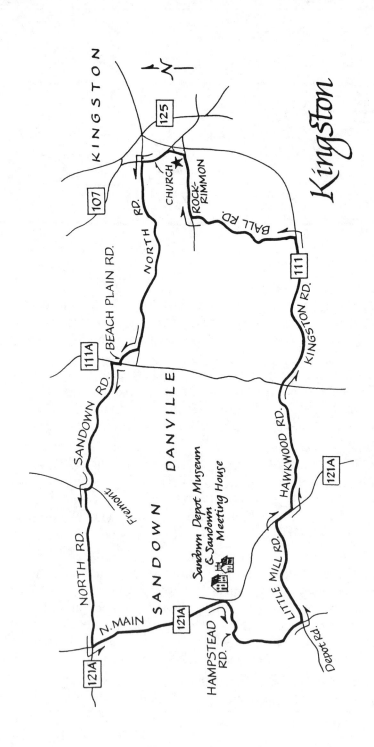

Kingston

turning leaves, (often dancing across your path), virtually no traffic, and the classic beauty of New England backroads.

This is a super family ride—for older children. It is hilly, so make sure they're ready for it. Let them walk if they need to. You may want to plan a stop afterward at Kingston State Beach for swimming and picnicking.

RIDE INFORMATION

Highlights: One of the oldest towns in the state (Kingston), Josiah Bartlett House, Kingston State Beach.

Start: Kingston Village common. At the village common, park across the street from the fire station or on one of the side roads that intersect the common.

RIDE DIRECTIONS

0.0 **Start the ride from the fire station on Rockrimmon Road. From fire station, go left toward the gazebo.**
At 0.1 mile on left is the Josiah Bartlett House. This home has been continuously lived in by Bartlett's direct descendents, and until 1940 was an active, working farm. On the grounds is a linden tree planted by Dr. Bartlett. It is one of two such trees in Kingston. The other tree is outside Kingston's oldest house, which is part of the Kingston 1686 House Restaurant.

0.2 **Bear left with curve onto Church Street.**
A pizza place and ice cream store are here.

0.7 **Left on North Road.**

3.7 **Bear right on Beach Plain Road.**

4.2 **At stop sign T-intersection go right on Main Street/ Route 111A (unmarked) for 0.1 mile.**

4.3 **Left on Sandown Road. (Becomes N. Danville Rd.)**

6.4 **Turn right on Freemont Road for 0.1 mile.**

6.5   **Left on North Road.**
   If you happen to be in this area in early spring, you may be fortunate to cycle past a couple of bogs and catch the "peep, peep, peep" of the spring peeper frogs.

8.9   **At stop sign, left on North Main Street (Rte. 121A).**
   This road has a moderate volume of fast traffic and no breakdown lane. At about the 11.0-mile mark on left is the turn for the Sandown Depot Museum and the historic Sandown Meeting House. Both are on the National Register of Historic Places. (More information on these sites can be found in the Chester-Sandown tour.)

11.1   **Right on Hampstead Road.**

11.8   **Y-intersection, bear left, still on Hampstead Road.**

13.1   **Left on Little Mill.**

14.8   **At stop sign, go right on South Main Street (Rte. 121A) for 0.3 miles.**
   Road has moderate traffic, no breakdown.

15.1   **Left on Hawkewood Road.**

17.1   **At stop sign at intersection, cross Route 111A diagonally to the right. Left on Kingston Road.**
   Located at this intersection is Danville Village Market, where you can buy subs and sandwiches.

19.7   **Left on Ball Road.**

21.4   **At stop sign/T intersection, go right on Rockrimmon Road (unmarked).**

22.4   **You're back at the fire station.**
   To get to Kingston State Park from here, travel half a mile south (in the opposite direction of the gazebo).

35 PORTSMOUTH- SOUTH BERWICK, ME

31.7 miles
Moderately difficult, hilly

The oldest city in the state, Portsmouth, has a long history. As far back as 1630, sea-weary travelers disembarked on the west bank of the Piscataqua River to find the ground covered with wild strawberries. The thriving area now known as Portsmouth, was originally named Strawbery Banke. Strawbery Banke lives on in Portsmouth's restored historical district, its annual festivals, and colorful Prescott Park—a flower-lovers paradise.

This community initially supported itself by fishing and farming, but eventually turned to ship-building because of the ready supply of lumber and Portsmouth's excellent harbor.

Portsmouth's history is well-preserved in its many old buildings and colonial structures. Wealthy sea captains built finely detailed houses that grace the old cobblestoned sections of town and appear untouched by the passing of centuries. If time permits, take a tour of the Moffatt-Ladd House (1763), John Paul Jones House (1758), Rundlet-May House (1807), Wentworth Coolidge Mansion (1710), Governor John Langdon House (1784), or the Warner House (1716).

Although a relatively small city of 26,000 population,

which swells by the thousands in the summer, Portsmouth has much to boast—historic sites and landmarks, Strawbery Banke, whale watches, theater, the Children's Museum of Portsmouth, and outstanding restaurants. Known as the "Restaurant Capital of New England," the Portsmouth area offers a limitless variety of dining experiences with more than 100 restaurants.

A popular event is the annual Market Square Day held the second weekend in June. The fair features a street fair with 300 exhibits, a road race, concert, historic house tours, and fireworks. Then there's the Jazz Festival, Bow Street Fair, the U.S.S. Albacore submarine, Prescott Park Arts Festival, the Blessing of the Fleet, and more. (Call the Portsmouth Chamber of Commerce at 603 436-1118 for dates and/or information on attractions.)

The bike tour winds along the seacoast for awhile, then circles back on less-traveled inland roads through villages in Maine where expansive maples grace the lawns of stately older homes and classic New England churches with towering steeples.

RIDE INFORMATION

Highlights: Historic Seacoast town of Portsmouth, many historic homes, U.S.S. Albacore submarine, Fort McClary State Park for picnicking, historic North Cemetery, fabulous Portsmouth restaurants, great water views.

Start: Memorial Bridge in Portsmouth. Park in Strawbery Banke free parking lot. (Follow signs down Marcy Street across from Prescott Park). If that lot if full, you'll have to park in the parking garage on Hanover St. If you have a roof rack, remember to remove your bike before entering the garage.

RIDE DIRECTIONS

0.0   **Start at Memorial Bridge. (Walk your bike.) Cross the bridge on 1N.**

0.6   **At stop sign, turn right on Government St. Follow Route 103 signs.**

0.9   **At stop light, go straight —on Route 103. Caution: Railroad tracks at about 1.0 mile.**

1.1   **Go right by gas station—still on Route 103E.**

1.4   **At stop sign by gas station, turn right—still on Route 103E.**

        At 3.1 miles is the Fort McClary State Park picnic area on the left. Rest room facilities are available here.

        Shortly after the park on the right is Cap'n Simeon's—a yummy seafood restaurant.

8.9   **At stop sign/T-intersection, left on 1-A South in York, Maine.**

        Dignified older homes with expansive maples, and historic churches and buildings abound along this road.

10.2   **At stop light, turn left on Route 1S.**

10.6   **Right on Route 91N. Caution: At about 17.7 miles you begin a steep descent with curves, and then a stop sign.**

18.4   **At stop sign, go left on Route 236S.**

21.5   **Right on Route 103E through Eliot, Maine.**

25.8   **Straight on State Road (sign a block up.) This road becomes Dennett St. A Citgo station will be on your right, and a sign on the left indicates a turn for the post office.**

28.7   **Stay straight for a short stretch on 103.**

29.0   **Turn right on Old Post Road to stop sign. At stop sign, go straight across (carefully!) onto Rte. 1S.**

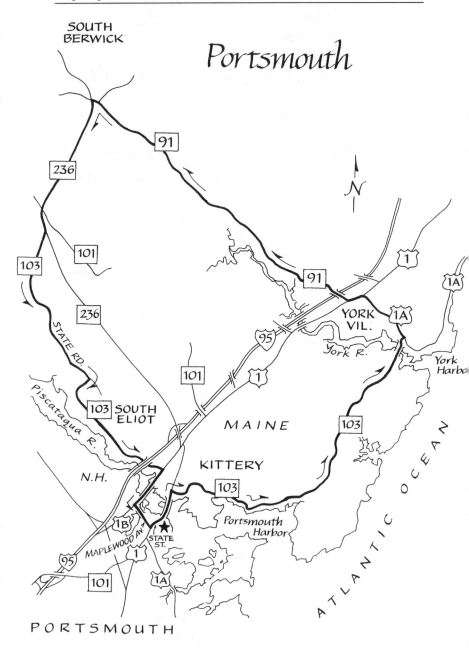

Portsmouth

SOUTH
BERWICK

(Route 1S loops under the bridge and brings you back up on the other side.) WALK YOUR BIKE ON THE SIDEWALK OVER THE BRIDGE. Riding it is prohibited.

At about 30.2 miles, a right turn takes you to the U.S.S. Albacore Park and Memory Garden. The vessel served as an experimental prototype for modern submarines. During its service from 1953-1972, it tested innovations in sonar, dive brakes, propellers, and controls. A short film is shown daily 9:30-5:30 during the summer. Adults $4.

30.4   Right on Maplewood Avenue exit to stop sign. Go right—still on Maplewood Avenue. Caution: Railroad tracks at 31.0 miles.

Historic North Cemetery on right at 30.9 miles. Signer of the Declaration of Independence, Governor John Langdon and signer of the Constitution, Captain Thomas Thompson of the Continental ship *Raleigh*, are among the noted citizens buried here. The cemetery was listed on the National Register in 1978.

31.3   Left on State Street.

31.7   Back at Prescott Park. (Then to wherever you parked your car.)

36 RYE-NEW CASTLE

22.7 miles
Mostly flat, a few short hills

Perhaps this tour should be called, "Scenic Ocean and Marsh Tour." Skirting nine miles of the 18 total miles of ocean shoreline in New Hampshire, this tour also cruises past marshland areas where an abundance of water birds exist—Great Blue Herons, sea gulls, mergansers, loons, and snowy white egrets. Do bring your camera along and capture some of New Hampshire's Seacoast wildlife on film.

Beginning at Odiorne Point State Park in Rye, wending through New Castle, touching a corner of Portsmouth, and back to Rye, the ride will meet your need for your "ocean fix." While at Odiorne, consider a stop at the Seacoast Science Center. Great for kids, but adults love it too. Explore seven different habitats within this 330-acre park. The ocean, shoreline, tidal pools, meadows, all offer a learning opportunity. Picnic areas, slides and swings, and miles of walking-biking trails also enhance the appeal of this park. The park also includes the remains of several pieces of American history—fishing encampments of the Penacook and Abenaki, explorations by Giovanni de Verrazano in 1524 to the still-standing, mysterious-looking camouflaged fortifications build during WWII.

Narrow streets with old houses flush to the curbs lend a

colonial air to New Castle, a small village of only 800 people, that was originally founded as a fishing village on Great Island in the late 1600s.

President Theordore Roosevelt made history here. He won a Nobel Peach Prize for work done in New Castle—in 1905 he negotiated the Treaty of Portsmouth, which ended the Russo-Japanese War.

Castlelike Wentworth-by-the-Sea Hotel is located on Rte. 1B in New Castle. Closed now, but with plans to be renovated and reopened, the structure was once a haunt for the rich and famous, and the site of the signing Russo-Japanese treaty.

The fall is a terrific time to ride this tour, as many hardwood trees line the streets you'll be riding through in Rye, New Castle, and Portsmouth. Large maples shade front yards and create lacy canopies as you ride past. Stone walls, grazing horses, and pricey estates also capture your attention along the way. In historic Rye Center, a 200-year-old Congregational church resides along with elegant colonial homes, and the newly renovated Rye Public Library.

Cycling along Rte. 1 (Ocean Blvd.) affords clear views of the Isles of Shoals, a string of small islands 10 miles off Portsmouth Harbor. Most of the islands, which are hardly larger than overgrown boulders, are owned by Maine. The best known, Appledore, is home to a marine lab.

RIDE INFORMATION

Highlights: A beauty of a tour that takes in ocean views, water birds, colonial homes, glimpses of pricey Seacoast estates, and a possible side trip to historic Wentworth-Coolidge Mansion.

Start: Odiorne Point State Park on Rte. 1A in Rye. Cost during the season is $2.50 a person, kids under 12 free. Park in lot.

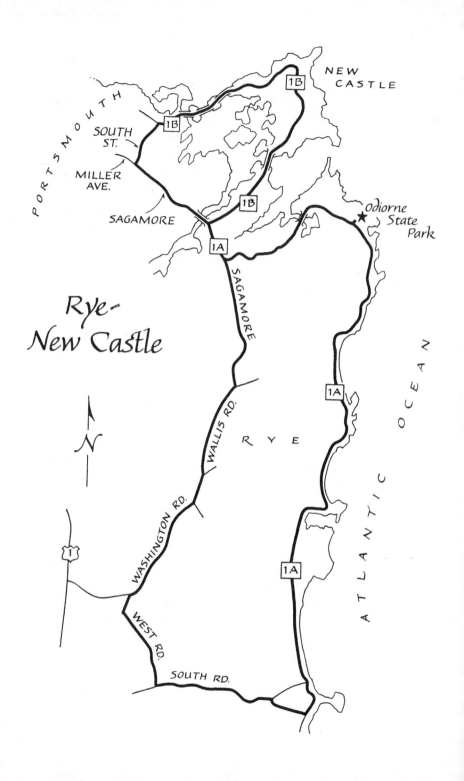

RIDE DIRECTIONS

0.0   **Right out of Odiorne entrance on Rte. 1A north.**

1.8   **At stop sign, continue on Rte. 1A.**

2.3   **Right on Rte. 1B north.**
A Great Blue Heron was fishing in the pond on the left after the turn on the day we pedaled past.

3.4   **Caution! Steel-grid draw bridge. Walk your bike.**
At 3.6 miles is Wentworth-by-the-Sea Hotel.

6.7   **At curve to right, go straight on New Castle Ave.**

6.8   **Left on South St.**

7.2   **At stop light, go left on Miller Ave.**
At 7.7 miles, a left on Little Harbor Rd. will bring you to the Wentworth-Coolidge Mansion, a rambling 42-room structure that overlooks Little Harbor. Considered to be one of the most significant houses of America's colonial era with unusual architecture from 1690-95, it was the official Royal Governor's residence.

8.2   **Caution! Another steel-grid bridge. Walk your bike.**

8.9   **Right on Sagamore by Mobil station.**

10.4   **At stop sign by Mobil station, go right on Wallis Rd. (unmarked).**
At 11.2 miles on the right, surrounded by a picket fence, is a colonial cape built in 1765, the Joseph Rand house. Note the field stone foundation.

For antique lovers, stop in at Antiques at Rye on your right at 11.4 miles.

Some multi-million dollar, palatial homes line this street as you follow it out to the ocean.

11.5   **Stay straight on this road by the junior high school. You'll now be on Washington Road.**
Soon you'll past through historic Rye Center—

by the white colonial church and town hall.

11.9   **At Y-intersection by the church, stay straight, to continue on Washington Road (unmarked).**

13.3   **Left on West Rd.**

Christine's Crossing is located at this turn—a unique store with unusual clothing and accessories. Worth stopping in.

14.5   **Left on South Rd.**

16.0   **At Y and stop sign, bear left—still on South Rd., and follow it to the ocean.**

16.4   **Left on Rte. 1A (Ocean Blvd.). The ocean!**

There are numerous places to stop and grab a bite to eat or an ice cream cone along Rte. 1A.

Jennis Beach has rest rooms.

22.7   **Right into Odiorne State Park.**

37 STRATHAM-RYE

26.3 miles
Mostly flat, a few short hills

New Hampshire's Seacoast is where the state began over 350 years ago. Although New Hampshire lays claim to only 18 miles of seacoast, most of it is public land and available for bathing, jogging, surfing, sailing, whatever. Just off shore is the historic (and somewhat mysterious) Isles of Shoals. In Portsmouth Strawbery Banke's public gardens are an oasis of color. Opportunities also abound for fine dining, whale watches, strolling through historic sea captains' homes, or participating in special days like Portsmouth's Jazz festivals, chili cook-offs, and outdoor summer theater.

Cruising through the quiet bedroom communities of Stratham, North Hampton, and Rye, this ride offers excellent scenery and some unexpected surprises. For example, as you pedal along the swamp land on Lovering Road in North Hampton, which parallels nearby I-95, who would think that wildlife would flourish so close to a busy thoroughfare? But it does. Early in the morning you can sometimes observe elusive deer grazing in the field, painted turtles sunning on rocks, and of course red-winged black birds darting among marsh reeds.

Continuing on the ride, you'll soon encounter the sparkling ocean in all its majesty. In Rye you cycle through the

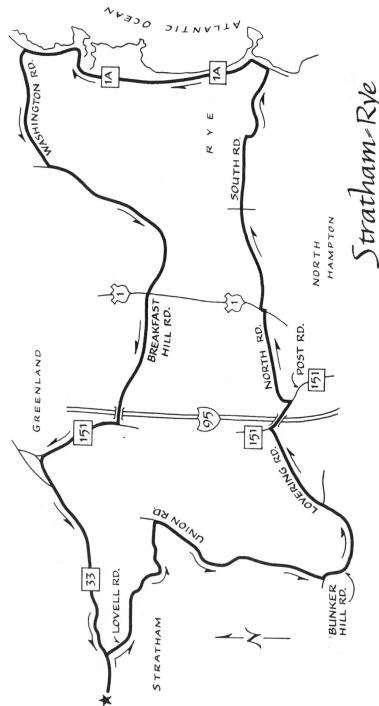

Stratham–Rye

ATLANTIC OCEAN

1A

1A

WASHINGTON RD.

RYE

SOUTH RD.

1

1

BREAKFAST HILL RD.

NORTH RD.

POST RD.

NORTH HAMPTON

151

GREENLAND

95

151

151

LOVERING RD.

UNION RD.

151

33

LOVELL RD.

BUNKER HILL RD.

STRATHAM

N

★

historic village center. A 200-year-old Congregational church resides here along with historic colonial homes, and the newly renovated Rye Public Library.

A bit busier traffic-wise than most rides in this book, this tour is nevertheless worth the effort. A popular tourist destination, the Seacoast of New Hampshire is a jewel worth adding to your treasure trove of experiences. Enjoy the ride.

RIDE INFORMATION

Highlights: A beauty of a tour that takes in ocean views, rural roads, glimpses of pricey Seacoast estates, and quite possibly wildlife sightings.

Start: Stratham Hill Park is 1.9 miles east of the Stratham Circle on Rte. 33E, on right.

RIDE DIRECTIONS

0.0 **Right out of the park on Rte. 33E.**
A very busy, fast-trafficked road, but with a nice breakdown lane. You won't be on it long.

The park has picnic tables and a covered pavilion, so bring a picnic lunch!

0.6 **Right on Lovell Road.**

1.4 **Right on Willow Brook Ave.**

1.9 **At stop sign/T intersection, left on High Street.**

2.6 **Right on Union Road.**

3.8 **At stop sign continue straight, still on Union Road.**
At 4.1 miles is Mill Valley Farm, where they sell yummy, organically grown vegetables.

At 4.5 miles, animal lovers note Rolling Meadow Pet Cemetery on the left. This pet resting place is managed by NHSPCA in Stratham, a wonderful organization for matching animals with owners.

5.0 **Left on Bunker Hill Road.**

6.0 **When the road curves to the right, stay straight on**

Lovering Road.
Marshes along this road are teeming with turtles, huge frogs, and ducks. Deer have also been sited.

7.5   **Right on Post Road (Rte. 151S). Cross over I-95.**

7.8   **Left on North Road.**

9.1   **Left on Rte. 1. This is a very busy road. Be careful! (But you'll only be on it for .1 of a mile.)**

9.2   **Right on North Road (continuing). North Road becomes South Road when you cross into Rye.**
Some multi-million dollar, palatial homes line this street as you follow it out to the ocean.

11.9   **At stop sign, continue straight on South Road.**

12.4   **Left on Rte. 1A (Ocean Blvd.). The ocean!**
There are numerous places to stop and grab a bite to eat or an ice cream cone along Rte. 1A.

At 13.0 miles, Jennis Beach has rest rooms.

15.5   **Left on Washington Road.**

17.0   **Bear left at stop sign to continue on Washington Road. (Rye Junior High will be on your right.)**
Soon you'll be in the historic center of Rye—by the white colonial church and town hall.

17.4   **Stay straight at fork, to continue on Washington Road.**
At 18.6 miles, a convenient store is on your right.

19.6   **Cross Rte. 1 to Breakfast Hill Road.**
Artichokes, a terrific gourmet food, wine shop, and kitchen accessories store, is at this corner.

21.3   **At stop sign, go right on Rte. 151.**

22.4   **Stay right, still on Rte. 151 to light.**
For super pizza and subs, stop at the Greek-owned Greenland House of Pizza on your right at 22.6 miles, or Ozzy's for terrific sandwiches on the right at Rte. 151.

22.8   **At the stop light, turn left on Rte. 33.**
        This road has fast traffic.

26.3   **Left at Stratham Hill Park.**

38 HAMPTON BEACH-EXETER

20.2 miles
Mostly flat, a few short hills

Although this ride bears all the earmarks of a classic New England bike ride—stone walls, apple orchards in bloom, pastoral scenery, and ocean views—it is not a good choice for the timid rider. Some of the roads on this tour are busy with traffic, depending on when you ride. So keep that in mind and if you're a newbie rider, do this ride during a weekday morning or early in the spring.

For the more seasoned rider or more adventurous, confident rider, this is a tour worth repeating. Beginning at Hampton's North Beach, the ride rolls through Hampton Falls, Exeter, Stratham, and back to the ocean at North Beach.

The apple orchards along the way present a colorful display of pink blossoms in the spring, or in the fall, the sweet smell of ripe apples tempt you to stop in, pick some apples, and dream about a pie later—a reward for the riding workout!

Nothing beats the ocean views as you near the shore along Atlantic Avenue. The elevated panoramic shots of the awesome Atlantic Ocean are a trip highlight.

One last thought—don't miss Kennedy's Restaurant. It's

an age-old landmark in Hampton, and by all means a "must-do" for ice cream. You can have lunch there before you leave on your ride, and when you're done, treat yourself to their terrific ice cream.

RIDE INFORMATION

Highlights: Apple orchards, pastoral farm scenes, ocean views, old graveyards, stone walls, easy riding.

Start: North Beach in Hampton. At Rte. 1 (Ocean Blvd.) and Rte. 27 (High St.).

RIDE DIRECTIONS

0.0 **Head west on Rte. 27 (High St.).**
Kennedy's Restaurant is at this intersection. Great for lunch or ice cream.

2.3 **Stop light at Rte. 1. Stay straight on Rte. 27W. Caution. Very busy intersection.**

2.8 **Left on Towle Farm Rd.**
At 2.9 miles there's a convenience store. Across from it is a pond and relaxation area.

4.9 **At stop sign/T intersection, right on Brown Rd. (unmarked).**
Apple trees line both sides of the road.

5.6 **At stop sign, right on Rte. 88 (unmarked).**
At 7.2 miles on the left is Red Barn Antiques. The Tilton House, a Federal-style colonial home with a center chimney built in 1740, is also here.

9.1 **Right on Rte. 27. (Busy road, but has a wide breakdown lane.)**

9.8 **Left on Guinea Rd.**

10.6 **At stop sign/V-intersection, go right on Stratham Heights Rd. (unmarked). A stone wall is at this turn.**

11.9 **Right on Bunker Hill Rd.**

14.3 **At T-intersection yield sign, go right on Post Rd.**

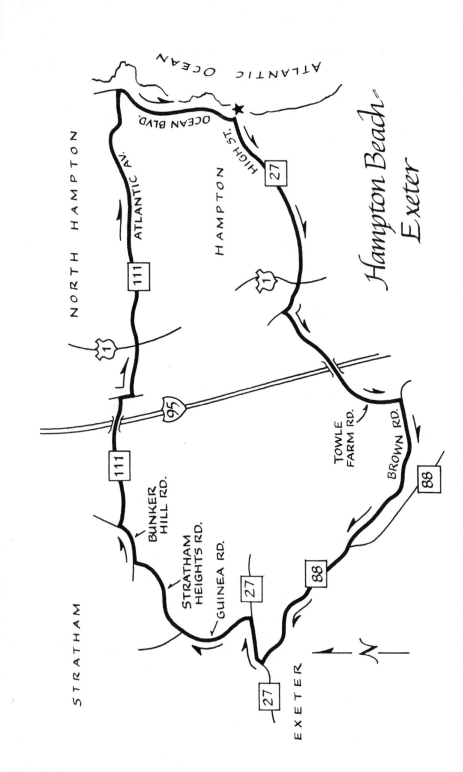

Hampton Beach—
Exeter

(Rte. 151, unmarked).

14.4   **Left on Rte. 111E (Atlantic Ave.) by the church. Stay on Rte. 111E all the way to the ocean.**

At Rte. 111 and Rte. 1 is Ronaldo's Restaurant in the plaza. Excellent Italian food.

At 15.5 miles Joe's Meat Market is worth a stop. Fresh produce and delightful homemade pies and pastries.

Along Atlantic Ave. you'll see very exclusive Seacoast estates, and as you near Atlantic avenue, breath-taking ocean views!

18.5   **Right on Rte. 1-A (Ocean Blvd.).**

An ice cream stop is in order at the 19-mile point.

And don't miss the multi-million dollar ocean-front homes along this road.

20.2   **Back where you began.**

39 HAMPTON FALLS-KENSINGTON

9.7 miles
Rolling with a few moderate hills

A lthough lesser-known areas of New Hampshire, Hampton Falls and Kensington are nevertheless blessed with some terrific roads for bike riding.

The canopy of tall trees, coupled with the lichen-covered stone walls along these country back roads quickly ease stress and replace it with an inner calm. Soon the apple orchards and bright, white horse paddocks that you're zipping past, remind you of what a gift it is to live in New Hampshire—or if you're visiting, why you came here in the first place. It is the perfect fall foliage tour.

Hampton Falls is known for its antique shops. You can find anything from conventional antique item here to unusual architectural appointments—such as balusters, carved doors, and stained glass windows. Be sure to check out Raspberry Farm (do indulge!) and its 200-year-old barn.

Kensington is a bedroom community that offers many less-traveled roads for cycling. Nearby is Seabrook, where you can visit the Science and Nature Center on Rte. 1 at Seabrook Station. Here, the kiddies can observe aquariums with live sea life or explore a salt marsh on a self-guided tour.

RIDE INFORMATION

Highlights: Short ride. Good for early in the season. Apple orchards and raspberry farms for picking. Historic buildings. Scenic—duck ponds, cows grazing, picturesque farm properties. Antique shops and the ocean nearby.

Start: Hampton Falls Town Hall. From Rte. 1, take Rte. 88W for .6 miles. Town hall on left.

RIDE DIRECTIONS

0.0   **Leave town hall parking lot, turn right on Route 88E.** Hampton Falls Town Hall, a two-story structure with simple Palladian windows, was built in 1877. Restorations 20 years ago uncovered original two-armed, gas lights with etched glass globes. They were then wired for electricity and currently grace the meeting room. Also in this room is an antique Seth Thomas clock. Original deacons benches also add charm to the colonial starkness of this building.

Across the street is the Hampton Falls Free Library, constructed in 1901. Inside a chandelier, which used to grace the foyer of the town hall, adds to the beauty of the exterior Corinthian columns and exquisite stained glass elliptical fanlight with sidelights.

0.1   **Left on Brown Road.** Photo op: Don't miss the duck ponds with accommodating subjects for photographs. Also wonderful, comfortable old farm houses dot this road, where Holstein cows teach subtle lessons about life's busyness... And, depending on the time of year, you may encounter the apple trees in glorious bloom, or smell the sweet, ripe fruit, ready for picking.

1.9   **At stop sign, right on Route 88W (unmarked).**

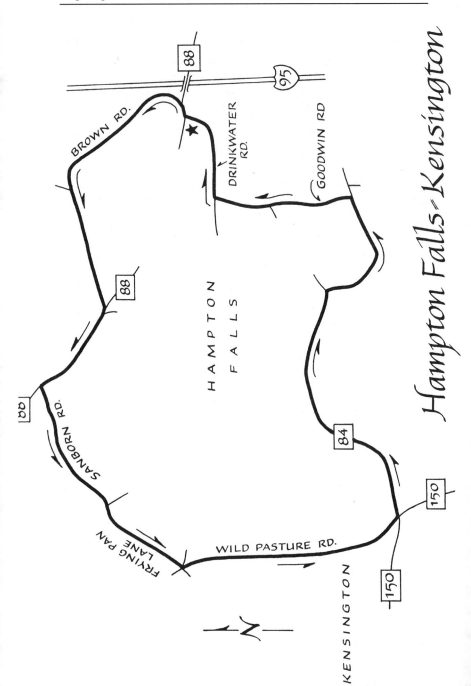

Hampton Falls-Kensington

At 2.5 miles on the right is Applecrest Farm. Pick some apples and make a pie for your grandmother!

2.6   **Left on Sanborn Road.**
You'll love this road. No traffic. The scent and sight of the towering evergreen trees and hardwood trees throwing lacy patterns in your path. Stone walls. And a chance to see some pricey, upscale homes.

3.5   **At T, right on Frying Pan Lane.**

4.0   **CAUTION—road becomes gravel for .1 mile.**

4.1   **Cross the tarred road and go left on Wild Pasture Road.**

5.6   **At stop sign, left on Route 84E. (This is a weird little jog.)**
At 6.7 miles, you can visit the Raspberry Farm. Pick your own raspberries, strawberries and blackberries from June to mid-October. The farm also features a 200-year-old historic barn. Purchase pies and tarts here if you'd rather not bake your own.

8.3   **Left on Goodwin Road.**

9.1   **At stop sign/T-intersection, right on Drinkwater Road (unmarked).**

9.7   **Left into town hall parking lot.**

40 PORTSMOUTH-NEWINGTON

14.0 miles
Mostly flat, a few short hills

Newington, New Hampshire is probably best known for its malls, Pease International Tradeport, and low taxes. But lesser known facts include that in 1710, the oldest town forest in the United States was established in Newington; that the Newington church bell (a gift from Newington, England) cracked in 1804 and had to be loaded on an oxen-drawn wagon, and hauled to Boston where Paul Revere recast the bell; and that it's home to a national treasure—the Great Bay Wildlife Refuge.

And one more lesser-known fact, that we hope remains a secret no longer, is that the new Rockingham Bicycle-Pedestrian Bridge that spans the Spaulding Turnpike connecting Pease International Tradeport to Portsmouth is open! Much work has been done by SABR (Seacoast Area Bicycle Routes), the City of Portsmouth, and the Pease Development Authority to make this a reality. The bridge is finally completed—and this ride takes you there.

Also consider a side trip to Red Hook Ale Brewery, a micro-brewery located on Pease. Known for its quirky ales and porters, Red Hook is partially owned by Anheuser-Busch. Red Hook offers tours where you can watch the bottling and brewing process, and of course, sample the results. Admission for the hour-long guided tour is $1.

The restaurant is worth a stop also. Food is reasonably priced and quite tasty. Worth the stop!

On this loop ride you will soon forget you're near a major population center as you cruise past apple orchards, cows and horses grazing lazily in nearby fields, lichen-covered stone walls, and ponds teeming with wildlife. Best thing to do is sit back and enjoy the ride.

RIDE INFORMATION

Highlights: New Rockingham Bicycle-Pedestrian bridge. Great Bay Wildlife Refuge a short side trip. Pleasant scenery. Most of the ride has little auto traffic. Redhook Ale Brewery for lunch or tour.

Start: New bus terminal, and park & ride in Portsmouth on Rte. 33 just west of I-95 access ramps.

RIDE DIRECTIONS

0.0   **Right out of the entrance to the park and ride on Rte. 33. Start your odometer here.**

0.4   **Right on Portsmouth Ave. (unmarked). Across from Sonoco station.**

1.1   **Right on Newington Rd.**
This road offers blooming apple orchards, horses and cows munching in the field, stone walls, corn fields. A relaxing, quiet road.

4.7   **At stop sign, left on Little Bay Rd.**
At 5.7 miles don't miss the delightful pine grove and the stately birch interspersed in this forested area.

5.9   **Right on Fox Point Road.**
At 6.0 miles is a quiet pond perfect for a picnic or a photo of ducks and other wildlife.

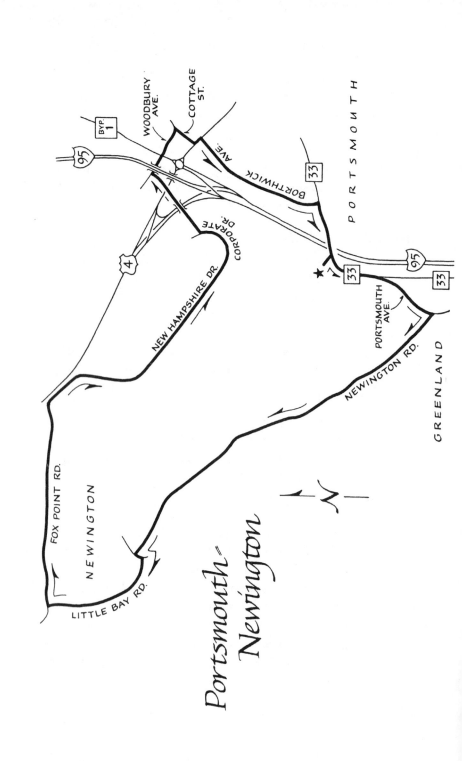

Portsmouth-
Newington

6.8 At stop sign cross over Nimble Hill Road to continue on Fox Point Rd.

> To visit the Great Bay Wildlife Refuge, take a right on Nimble Hill Road for a mile or so. The building is on your right. The refuge attracts loon, osprey, terns, harriers (marsh hawks), peregrine falcons, and is a winter roosting spot for bald eagles. Common song birds and wild turkeys abound. Coyote, red and gray fox, white-tailed deer, fish, and other mammals are also frequently sighted. This 1,054-acre refuge bordering Pease International Tradeport, has a number of trails open to the public.

7.3 Straight on Fox Point Rd. extension. It's a short bike-pedestrian pathway.

7.5 Left on Arboretum Dr. (unmarked), which becomes New Hampshire Dr., and then curves gently to the left and becomes Corporate Dr.

> You've entered Pease International Tradeport, home to numerous public and private sector organizations, and a focal point in the recovery of the Seacoast's regional economy. Military cutbacks forced Pease Air Force Base to close in 1991, but its transformation to an international tradeport continues to attract industry with total employment projected to be more than 4,000 within five years.

> Take a side trip down Corporate Dr. to Red Hook Ale Brewery for a tour—or lunch if you're hungry—they make a mean hamburger.

10.7 Right over bridge—hang on—the "real" bridge is yet to come!

11.1 Right on paved pathway with wood railings. The bike-pedestrian bridge appears momentarily.

11.4 End of pathway. Take a short right to stop sign.

11.5   At stop sign, go right on Woodbury Ave. (unmarked). You will immediately go under a concrete overpass.

11.9   Right on Cottage St. to stop light. At stop light, go left one block, then right on Borthwick Ave.
Caution! Railroad tracks at 13.3 miles.

13.5   At stop sign, left to Rte. 33, then right on Rte. 33.

14.0   Right into entrance of the bus terminal/park & ride.

I want a "Bicycle NH" T-shirt!

Bicycling Southern New Hampshire

Top quality preshrunk 100% cotton T-shirt. Vibrant colors—teal, purple, fuchsia and black—on gray or white T-shirt. Large or XL only. Shirts are $16 each, plus shipping ($3 for first shirt, $1. for each additional.)

(See order form on page 223.)

Other Great Books by Nicolin Fields Publishing, Inc.

You can find these books at your local book store, Amazon.com, or if you'd rather order by phone or mail, see page 223.

The Cohos Trail The Guidebook to NH's Great Unknown by Kim Robert Nilsen

Hikers from all over are discovering the newly developed Cohos Trail which covers 160 miles of NH's far-northern Coos County, where moose reign and only loons break the grand mountain silence. 240 pages. Index. Photos. Maps. $17.95

Seven Large, Detailed Maps of the Cohos Trail by Kim Robert Nilsen

Perfect to enhance your wilderness hiking experience. $10.

Bicycling Southern NH by Linda Chestney

Newly revised and expanded second edition of this popular book, which you now hold in your hands! $17.95

Bicycle Across America by Barbara Siegert

A guide to five classic cross-country adventures. Includes preparation tips, maps, and tour notes. Dare to go the distance! 208 pages. $14.95

Mountain Biking New Hampshire's State Parks and Forests by Linda Chestney

NH boasts 164,000 acres of state parks, forests, nature areas, and reservoirs—a mecca for mountain bike adventures. These trail rides deliver just what you expect from New Hampshire—beautiful wilderness and classic New England scenery. Route notes and maps. 176 pages. $14.95

Medicinal Herbal Therapy A Pharmacist's Viewpoint by Steven Ottariano, R.Ph.

New choices in drug-free remedies—natural healing from medicinal herbs. Registered pharmacist, Steve Ottariano, offers a balanced perspective on traditional Western medicine and complementary treatments. 192 pages. Index. Appendixes. $14.95

A Little Kinder Than Necessary A Collection of Character-Building Secrets by Beth Taber

"Words of wisdom, gathered into a delightful bouquet, bunched with charming illustrations... you'll find that the pages of this book please the eyes and challenge the soul. I enjoyed every one." Kaye Cook, Ph.D., psychologist, professor, author, mother of two. 96 pages, 6" x 6" Illustrated. $9.95

Order Form

(Please photocopy)

Name_____

Address_____

City_____

Phone_____

Email_____

Send check or money order to:
Nicolin Fields Publishing, Inc.
3 Red Fox Road
North Hampton, NH 03862

Credit card orders, please call: 800 431-1579

T-Shirt

Color (choose one): ____Gray ____White
Number of shirts: _____ Size (circle one): Large XL
Shirt total ($16 each)   _____
Shipping ($3. first, $1 each addl.)   _____

Books

__Bicycle Across America, $14.95   _____
__Mountain Biking NH State Parks, $14.95   _____
__Medicinal Herbal Therapy, $14.95   _____
__A Little Kinder Than Necessary, $9.95   _____
__Bicycling Southern NH, $17.95   _____
__The Cohos Trail, $17.95   _____
Shipping, $4 first book, $1. each addl.)   _____

Maps

__Seven Detailed, Large Cohos Trail Maps, $10.   _____
Shipping, maps, $2.   _____

Total enclosed: _____
(Questions? Call 603 964-1727)

About the Author

Linda Chestney has spent two thirds of her life on the saddle of a bike. She began her cycling career on a red Schwinn with no gears. But in the flat plains of the Upper Midwest you don't need much more. Schooling and family eventually brought her to the East Coast.

She now puts thousands of miles on her sport touring bike while cycling the backroads of New England. Her red Schwinn was upgraded years ago, and these days a sleek, royal blue, metallic 21-speed Terry stands at-the-ready in the garage.

Chestney, a professional writer who has published magazine articles locally, regionally, and nationally, has been writing since high school. She's also worked in the public relations field for 18 years.

She holds a degree in Interior Design from Chamberlayne Jr. College in Boston, a B.A. in Psychology from Gordon College in Wenham, Massachusetts, where she also concentrated in journalism, and a master's degree in nonfiction writing from the University of New Hampshire.

A "newcomer" New Englander of 26 years, Chestney was originally a "flatlander" from South Dakota. She returns occasionally to the Midwest to see relatives, check out the cowboy boots, and bring back a tumbleweed or two. She resides on the Seacoast of New Hampshire with her husband and three pooches. Their house is tucked in the woods where deer and cross-country skiers roam.